FUTURE
MAKING

green press INITIATIVE

FUTURE MAKING

Getting Your Organization Ready for What's Next

Clark A. Murdock

Murdock Associates, Inc.
Stevensville, Maryland

All proceeds from the sale of this book will be donated to organizations helping recent veterans struggling with psychological problems stemming from their service to the country.

The author gratefully acknowledges the generous contribution of the Smith Richardson Foundation to the publication of this book.

Printed in the United States of America

ISBN 978-0-9797810-0-1
Library of Congress control number 2007905035

Published by **Murdock Associates, Inc.**
Stevensville, Maryland 21666
For further information, visit **murdockassociatesinc.com.**

Contents

Preface

At any one time, about a third of the Fortune 500 firms will not exist in seven years.[1] *Future Making* is about improving the odds that your organization will last.

The purpose of this book is to help real people—both those who make decisions for organizations and those who support them—do a better job of coping with change and uncertainty. Organizations can't literally make *the* future, but they can make *their* future. Or, like many in the dot.com implosion that began in mid-2000, they can fail to make their futures.

This book is intended primarily for those in larger organizations (hundreds of members and more) that must change to ensure that their future products, services, and capabilities are relevant to future demand. It provides advice to an organization's senior management—CEOs and their equivalents, COOs, CFOs, executive vice presidents, and others—on how they can *make decisions* and *take actions* today that better position their organizations for the future. But anyone leading an organization or contemplating a start-up can benefit from this approach.

I have been fascinated with how organizations make decisions for my entire professional career. I wrote my first book on then-Defense Secretary Robert S. McNamara's effort to impose, on a decidedly unruly institution, decision-making processes and products that he had employed during his private sector career. This book distills what I learned from two decades of advising, assisting, or planning for top-level officials in the Office of the Secretary of Defense, the CIA, the National Security Council, the House Armed Services Committee, and the Air Force. These lessons learned have been tested and refined further since I left the government and started my private consulting practice.

So what can an old Washington hand tell someone in the private sector about planning for the future? An organization cannot make its future unless those at the top make the tough decisions, and over the last two-plus decades, I have learned much, often the hard way, about how to influence my bosses' actions and help them make those decisions—a skill needed in any organization, public or private.

My five years at the Pentagon as the top civilian strategic planner for the Air Force (I had five generals as my immediate boss during that time) were the most challenging and rewarding of my career. It was also when I began to formulate my ideas about Future Making. General Ronald R. Fogleman became Chief of Staff of the Air Force in October 1994, and stated from the outset that he was determined to change the Air Force to meet the emerging realities of the post-Cold War era. He sparked a debate on how the Air Force should organize itself for change, and, in Washington terms, I prevailed: my recommendation that General Fogleman appoint a special assistant for long-range planning was adopted, and I became the civilian deputy. Our job was to help the Air Force develop a coherent, shared strategic vision for the future Air Force and then to institutionalize a long-range planning process. [2]

Most observers agree that the early Fogleman years were enormously creative ones for the Air Force. The new strategic vision that emerged, *Global Engagement: A Vision for the 21st Century Air Force* (October 1996), has been an enduring legacy. Many initiatives begun during that time have contributed significantly to the Air Force's astonishing successes in Kosovo and Afghanistan. The success of the Air Force's efforts to transform itself to meet the new post-Cold War challenges has been demonstrated where it counts—namely, in the battlespace. In short, the Air Force has been making its future.

As I helped the Air Force make its future, I learned that much of what I did to foster future-oriented change did not fit the usual job description of a planner. In fact, much of what passed for planning (including some planning processes and products that I had a big hand in designing) actually made it harder for the Air Force to change. It was my experience that too many planners, both in and out of government, acted as if planning were an end in itself, and that it was successful if it produced a good plan. Whether the organization actually changed as a result was beside the point.

As I wrote the initial draft of this book while I was teaching at the National War College during 2000, I closely followed the travails of companies as they rose and (all too frequently) fell in a very turbulent market. I realized that what I was really thinking and writing about was not planning per se, but *how organizations can (but often do not) change to better position themselves for the future.* I still use the term "planner" as it makes a better title than "futures guy" or "inter-temporal change expert"; but *Future Making* is the construct for understanding how to help organizations change.

After a decade in academia and two decades in the U.S. government, I became a consultant in January 2001, and also joined the staff of a non-partisan think tank, the Center for Strategic and International Studies (CSIS). While my draft manuscript sat on the shelf gathering dust (like most strategic plans), I found that ideas and words from my book resonated with my clients and, in fact, helped me get new clients, including a big one in December 2005 (that is, IBM). To me, this was the final validation—ideas that I first put down on paper during 2000 were making me money in the new millennium. Once I knew that future-making ideas and words "worked," I realized that I needed to go back and finish my book, because that might help me get more business (see ClarkMurdock.com for corporate off-site options). I hope that you will find *Future Making: Getting Your Organization Ready for What's Next* an entertaining and informative read—it has helped me make my future, and I believe it will help you make yours.

Notes

1 Charles Handy, "Finding Sense in Uncertainty," Rowan Gibson (Ed), *Rethinking the Future.* London: Nicholas Brealoy Publishing, LTD, 1997), 17.

2 For an assessment of how effectively the Air Force's senior management team (supported by its strategic planning office) made its future, see Michael Barzelay and Colin Campbell, *Preparing for the Future: Strategic Planning in the U.S. Air Force* (Washington, D.C.: Brookings Institution Press, 2003).

Acknowledgments

This book is personal to me. As I said earlier, it is grounded in my experience. But it is personal in a broader sense because it is my conviction, not one shared by most political scientists, that personalities really matter. How an individual does his or her job makes a big difference in how organizations behave. Moreover, people can learn and can change how they do their jobs. I am a prime example.

This book has evolved as I have learned more about Future Making. Ideas first developed in the Air Force have changed as I have applied them in my consulting practice. They have also changed in response to the reactions of my first readers—Vernon Guidry, my wife Kathleen, Leslie Lewis, Steve Corrick, Kate Briggs, Woody Briggs, Bob Trice, Tom Wilkerson, and John Milam. Their support helped me believe in the book; their suggestions made it a better book.

I would also like to take this opportunity to thank Ron Fogleman who, as Chief of Staff of the United States Air Force, first empowered me as a planner in his Air Force. I have greatly appreciated the opportunity to serve the nation by working for the Air Force and am profoundly grateful to the Air Force for giving me a home and a role to play.

I would also like to thank Vernon Guidry—colleague, friend, collaborator, and co-conspirator. Without Vernon, I wouldn't have learned some of the things I did; I couldn't have written the book that I have.

I also owe personal thanks to Marin Strmecki, Vice President of the Smith Richardson Foundation. He has believed in the book since he read the draft manuscript in 2004 and kept reminding me that I needed to return to it. Smith Richardson gave me a small grant in 2006 to update and revise the book—a decision that, once I accepted the money, provided the final push I needed to complete the job.

To express my great admiration and gratitude for the men and women who serve in this nation's armed forces, all proceeds from the sale of this book will be donated to organizations helping recent veterans struggling with psychological problems stemming from their service to the nation.

And finally, I would like to thank my wife, Kathleen. She has shared my life while I pursued, rather intensely, a pretty tumultuous career. Her love and support have helped me in ways I can't begin to enumerate. This book is dedicated to her. It also is dedicated to my children, Jesse, Jane and Carlos, and their children, Ross, Jack, Cameron, Finn and Piers. This book is in memory of Carlos—we'll always miss you—and in loving support of his wife, Heather.

1

Organizations Can Make
Their Futures

THE THESIS OF THIS BOOK is that organizations can, to a significant and useful degree, make their own futures. And they had better try. By definition, what works today is unlikely to work tomorrow. The future demand for your products, services, or capabilities will be different from today's demand. The issue is not whether your organization will have to change, but how much it will have to change to be relevant to future demand. Inactivity during an era of rapid change such as the one we are experiencing now is a recipe for disaster.

Organizations change as a result of decisions made by members of that organization. Evolutionary change usually reflects many small decisions made by those on the front lines—the organization as a system reacts and adapts to a changing environment. This works as long as the environment changes slowly. But today, the pace of change is too fast, its nature too discontinuous, and its extent too broad for incrementalism to work. Organizations have to make their futures happen or risk being overtaken by the future. *Future Making* is for organizations that are determined to last and are willing to take steps today to better position themselves to survive tomorrow.

I'm not, of course, talking about literally making the future in any macro sense. But organizations can make *their* futures by investing in new capabilities that will produce new services or products that might better meet future demand. The issue is what decisions to make. This book offers a guide to that crucial decision making. And decision making is the key to it all. Today, making a wrong decision is usually better than making no decision. A wrong decision can be reversed by another decision. There is no cure for indecisiveness.*

The usual tool for dealing with the future is the strategic plan, a device whose greatest utility in many organizations is that of a door stop. Why do so many strategic plans sit on the shelf gathering dust? Why is there such widespread disillusionment with strategic planning? Why does "organizational future making" sound like an oxymoron?

▲ **Most organizations fail to make real decisions about priorities and resources in their planning processes.**

Let me begin to answer that by offering this anecdote from a titan of the New Economy. Andrew Grove provides a fascinating account in his book, *Only the Paranoid Survive,* of how Intel transformed itself from a memory chip producer in a death spiral to the largest semiconductor company in the world. Grove recounts a mid-1985 conversation with the chairman and president, Gordon Moore:

> I asked, "If we got kicked out and the board brought in a new CEO, what do you think he would do?" Gordon answered without hesitation, "He would get us out of memories." I stared at him, numb, then said, "Why shouldn't you and I walk out the door, come back and do it ourselves."[1]

Grove then describes how hard it was to carry through this newly formed strategic intent, noting if they had "dithered longer" and "stayed indecisive," they would have followed other memory producers into oblivion.[2] Andrew Grove is clearly one of the most successful and decisive corporate leaders of the past decade, and yet even he concludes that in "looking back over my own career, I have never

---

* Organizations down to their last dime obviously don't have resources to invest in new capabilities. Nor can they afford another mistake. But most organizations are not at the end of their ropes and have the resources, if not the ability or will, to make their futures.

made a tough change, whether it involved resource shifts or personnel moves, that I haven't wished I had made a year or so earlier."[3]

On its face, this account of a seemingly casual but pivotal exchange may not seem to be an advertisement for formalizing a future-making process, but let's take a closer look. First, we are dealing with Grove and Moore, the author of Moore's Law (that the number of transistors on a chip doubles about every two years). At the time the reported conversation took place, few if any were better able to assess future trends of the new world that they were helping to create than this pair. Second, Grove found a rhetorical device to rid himself of the tyranny imposed by the demands and success of Intel's then-current business. He asked a "what if" question of particular pertinence to himself—what would his successor do? Finally, he acted decisively to position Intel to meet the future he and Moore forecast.

Grove was engaged in future making. I will return repeatedly to these themes in this book:

▲ First, make the best effort possible to understand what the future will demand. We will explore in this book ways to do this.

▲ Think in terms of end states—what the organization must achieve to be successful in the future—then plan backwards. It is much more productive than planning for an amorphous future.

▲ Finally, act decisively to move towards the new end states. Don't drag out your planning until it becomes posthumous. Act.

This is future making.

Most organizations, it is safe to say, will not have a Grove and a Moore together at the precise moments when these conversations about the future need to take place, but the conversations do need to take place. What are we to do? Creating an effective planning process that addresses the future-making precepts listed above could help senior management make future-oriented decisions. But all too often, planning seems to substitute talking for action.

▲
Decision Making Never Goes Out of Style

In the 1970s and 1980s, many of the "how to" manuals on strategic planning (of which *Future Making* is a latter day example), put decision making at the core of management. As Alan Walter Steiss flatly stated:

> Decision making is one of the most pervasive functions of management, whether in business or in government. If an organization is to achieve its objectives, decisions must be made, and action programs arising from these decisions must be implemented.[1]

In the 1990s, however, the role of the CEO as decision maker did not receive much attention. Instead, it was the CEO as leader, building (depending on the author) the quality company, the visionary company, the learning organization, the nimble organization, and so on.

Despite these fads about what CEOs should do, there were always hard-core traditionalists who stayed focused on decision making. For example, Michael E. Porter, the competition guru, argued that the key to creating sustainable market advantage is making "tough trade-off choices" and "strong leaders willing to make choices are essential.[2]

The CEO as chief decision maker, however, appears to be making a comeback in the business literature. Citing the now famous quote from Napoleon—"Nothing is more difficult, and therefore precious, than to be able to decide"—*Fortune* magazine devoted its June 27, 2005, edition to decision making. Before identifying the twenty "epic

Planning with No Beef

Let us now return to the questions posed above. Why do so many strategic plans sit on the shelf gathering dust? Why is there such widespread disillusionment with strategic planning? Why isn't future making an oxymoron?

These questions have a number of answers. The overarching reason is quite simple: most organizations fail to make real decisions about priorities and resources in their planning processes. The re-decisions" that shaped the modern world of business, Jerry Useem observed:

> For modern decidophobes, business is a bad hiding place. Strategies, careers, companies—they're all made of decisions the way glass is made of sand. The quality of your decisions is what makes you valuable. And the hardest ones roll uphill: A CEO's job, it's been said, is to make the decision that can't be delegated.[3]

In January 2006, *Harvard Business Review* also published a special issue on "Decision Making: Better>Faster>Smarter," in which editor Thomas A. Stewart stated succinctly that "decisions are the essence of management. They're what managers do—sit around all day making (or avoiding) decisions."[4] Similarly, Paul Rogers and Marcia Blenko wrote: "Decisions are the coin of the realm in business. Every success, every mishap, every opportunity seized or missed is the result of a decision that someone made or failed to make."[5]

---

1 Alan Walter Steiss, *Strategic Management and Organizational Decision Making* (Lexington, Mass: Lexington Books, 1985), 8.

2 Michael E. Porter, "What Is Strategy," *Harvard Business Review* (November-December 1996), 77.

3 Jerry Useem, "Decisions, Decisions" *Fortune* (June 27, 2005), Fortune Archive online version, 1.

4 Thomas A. Stewart, "Did You Ever Have to Make Up Your Mind?" *Harvard Business Review* (January 2006), 12.

5 Paul Rogers and Marcia Blenko, "Who Has the D? How Clear Decision Roles Enhance Organizational Performance," *Harvard Business Review* (January 2006), 53. ▲

sulting plans usually establish ambitious goals and milestones, with varying degrees of specificity, but rarely identify where the resources will come from to pay for them. It's relatively easy to reach agreement on new ventures and new plans; it's relatively hard to decide on what to *stop* doing. And unless the organization has infinite resources, it will be necessary to stop doing some things in order to put resources down on bets about the future.

It's always hard to make these tough decisions—that's why they are called tough—but it's even harder when your planning processes get in the way.* Planning is about setting priorities. When resource constraints are applied, those at the bottom of the priority pole don't get funded. A planning process that produces key decisions on where the firm is going and not going will have winners and losers. This is not easy or uncontroversial. There will be heated battles because those invested in the old or lower priority ways of doing business will fight for their survival. Serious future making is not a "feel good" exercise; it's about who will have a place, and how big that place will be, in the company's future.

Setting clear priorities among its activities is hard for any organization, because these choices often represent zero-sum, "win-lose" situations for the individual participants. Senior management doesn't like to make these decisions unless forced to. During the annual budget crunch they sometimes have to, because there are only so many dollars to dispense. However, during the *planning cycle,* they don't have to, because, as Yogi Berra observed, "the future ain't here yet." The temptation to kick the can down the road by postponing tough decisions about what to give up is usually too great. Michael Goold and John J. Quinn noted that in company after company, behavior that would be ridiculed in its budget control process—no clear agreement on objectives, no quantitative targets, no monitoring of progress—was routinely accepted in the strategic planning process.[4]

Planning without realistic resource constraints produces plans that are little more than unaffordable wish lists. They establish ends without means. They provide false empowerment because those charged or tasked to do something new aren't given additional resources to do the job. Then the implementers face the same questions that were ducked during the planning process: What do I stop doing in order to pay for this new initiative? Whose jobs do I eliminate to hire the people I need for these new tasks? Tough decisions just get

---

* Michael C. Mankins and Richard Steele argue that the ways in which companies do strategic planning are actually obstacles to decision making. Their survey found that "companies with standard planning processes and practices make only 2.5 major strategic decisions each year on average (by 'major,' we mean they have the potential to increase company profits by 10% or more over the long term)," compared to the 4.1 to 6.1 major decisions by companies that made decisions continuously. Mankins and Steele, "Stop Making Plans; Start Making Decisions," *Harvard Business Review* (January 2006), 76–84.

Avoiding the Trap of Indecision

I've had a lot of experience turning around troubled companies, and one of the first things I learned was that whatever hard or painful things you have to do, do them quick and make sure everyone knows what you are doing and why. Whether dwelling on a problem, hiding a problem, or dribbling out a partial solution to a problem while you wait for the high tide to raise your boat—dithering and delay almost always compound a negative situation. I believe in getting the problem behind me quickly and moving on.

—Lou Gerstner (former IBM CEO)
Who Says Elephants Can't Dance
(New York: Harper Business, 2002), 68

Decisiveness is the ability to make difficult decisions swiftly and well, and act on them. Organizations are filled with people who dance around decisions without ever making them. Some leaders simply do not have the emotional fortitude to confront the tough ones. When they don't, everybody in the business knows they are wavering, procrastinating, and avoid reality.

—Larry Bossidy (former CEO, Honeywell) & Ram Charan
Execution: The Discipline of Getting Things Done
(New York: Crown Business, 2002), 123

The Marine Corps battle this syndrome [decidophobia] with the "70% solution." If you have 70% of the information, have done 70% of the analysis, and feel 70% confident, then move. The logic is simple: A less than ideal action, swiftly executed, stands a chance of success, whereas no action stands no chance. The worst decision is to make no decision at all.

—Michael Useem
"Great Escapes", *Fortune* (June 27, 2005)
Fortune Archive online version, 1

They [competent CEOs] know and accept the surgeon's time-tested principle, the oldest principle of effective decision-making: A degenerative disease will not be cured by procrastination. It requires decisive action.

—Peter F. Drucker
"The Theory of Business,"
Harvard Business Review (September–October 1994)
as excerpted in "What Executives Should Remember,"
Harvard Business Review (February 2006), 147▲

tougher when they are up close and personal. "Business as usual" is the easy way out.

From this perspective, strategic plans become an embarrassment because they underscore the gap between what an organization says it wants to do and what it actually does. No one reads the dust-gathering plans because people don't like to be reminded of how far their actions fall short of their aspirations. Achievable goals become unachievable if an organization is unwilling to free up resources by ending lower priority activities. Plans become irrelevant because organizations fail to carry them out.

It is indisputable that many senior managers complain that strategic planning is a waste of time. That's because most senior managers aren't *serious* about strategic planning. During the planning process, they don't make tough decisions that trade off old ways of doing business for new ways. As a result, there's no beef in the plans.

The real building blocks of future making are decisions, which may or may not be made during a planning process and may or may not be embedded in a plan. As Harvard Business Review editor Thomas A. Stewart observed, "decision making is a kind of fortune-telling, a bet on the future."[5] Making tough decisions on what to do and what not to do. Easy to say; hard to do. Why is that the case?

Decision Avoidance—Let Us Count the Ways

Future making requires decision making. Organizations don't make decisions, however; *people occupying positions in the organization make decisions.* We humans resist change and duck tough decisions, particularly when they involve near-term costs suffered for long-term benefits. By its very nature, my concept of future making is about change: an organization figures out where it wants to be at some future point in time and decides what changes it has to make today in order to get where it wants to be tomorrow. The degree of change required of an organization is directly related to the difficulty of the decisions that must be made. Transforming a firm to meet the future demand for its products is much harder than reengineering a firm to improve its operational effectiveness.

The reasons why we humans resist making tough decisions and implementing change are almost endless: inertia; ingrained habits; vested in status quo; risk-averse; fear of unknown; "not-invented-here" syndrome; fear of failure; fear of accountability; and so on. Everybody knows change is inevitable, but planning for change is inherently uncomfortable for many people. For many, accepting the need to change means there is something wrong with what they are doing today. I once had a boss tell me that he did not like the "transformation word," because it seemed too critical of the status quo.

There's a cognitive dissonance associated with our reluctance to change. In private conversations, I've often had senior officials exclaim: "You're right. Damn it. You're right. We have to change that." And then the next day, even the next hour, continue to do exactly that which had to be changed. Their statements are not disingenuous; their failure to change is not malicious. They just fail to make the connection between what they know at some level and what they actually do.

The difficulty of taking ownership of the need to change clearly increases with age, seniority, and experience. Gary Hamel notes the inhibiting effect of the "tyranny of experience":

> Where are you likely to find people with the least diversity of experience, the largest investment in the past, and the greatest reverence for industrial dogma? At the top. And where will you find the people responsible for creating strategy? Again, at the top.
>
> The organizational pyramid is a pyramid of experience. But experience is valuable only to the extent that the future is like the past.[6]

I believe that from a psychological perspective, a non-serious, ineffective planning process offers relief to the change-averse CEO. He can claim he is trying to change the organization (hence, the strategic planning process) and has a scapegoat for the organization's failure to change (the incompetent strategic planner).

Many senior managers find it easier to hold their organizations accountable for the failure to change than to hold themselves personally accountable for failing to change. A comptroller can agree that

---

You Make Your Future One Big Decision at a Time

The Case of Apple's Steve Jobs:

Business Week on why Jobs was able to turn Apple around when he returned (after being fired 12 years earlier) in 1997:

> Jobs has applied his old strategy to the new digital world. With absolute control, breakout innovation, and stellar marketing, he has created products that customers lust after.

> "The great thing about Steve is that he knows that great business comes from great product. . . . First you have to get the product right, whether it's the iPod or an animated movie," said Peter Schneider, former chairman of Disney's studio.

> Time and again . . . Apple has eschewed calls to boost market share by making lower-end products or expanding into adjacent markets. . . . "I'm as proud of what we don't do as I am of what we do," Jobs often says.

Why Disney was able to buy Pixar from Apple:

> The deal came together on Internet time, in just three days. [Disney CEO] Iger wanted to show that Disney can be a nimble company, willing to embrace the latest digital technologies to deliver its content. "I think we impressed [Jobs and other Apple execs] with how quickly we could make a decision," said Iger.

On why Disney could move so fast:

> Among [Robert A.] Iger's first decisions [after taking over from long-time CEO Michael D. Eisner] was dismantling the corporate strategic planning operation Eisner often used to scuttle risky new plans.

Source: Excerpted from "Steve Jobs' Magic Kingdom: How Apple's demanding visionary will shake up Disney and the world of entertainment," *Business Week* (February 6, 2006), online version, Businessweek.com/magazine. ▲

---

his budgeting process is dysfunctional but he is helpless to change it because the firm won't change. This displacement is harder, of course, for those at the top of an organization who can change a company's strategy, direction, or future. But it is those at the top who may be least inclined to change.

All of us know that change is endemic, and we must change ourselves to meet shifting circumstances. One response to this dilemma is denial—as my good friend Vernon is fond of saying, "denial ain't just a river in Egypt." Another response is to step up to the plate and start future making.

Why Future Making?

The future is inevitable; it always comes. Like the last decade, it will bring more change and uncertainty, but the pace of change seems to be accelerating. Actions taken today have long-term consequences. Actions an organization could take today could better position it for the future. Waiting passively for the future to arrive will ensure that tomorrow's challenges will be met with today's capabilities. Not likely to work. The senior management of any organization, firm, or company needs to put the future on today's agenda.

A firm that doesn't try to make its future is in denial. The imperative for future making is even greater in a world operating at Internet speed, because the faster pace of change reduces the window of opportunity to make timely decisions. The time horizons differ depending on the nature of the business, of course, but at the heart of serious future making is the making of decisions that trade off current activities for activities that prepare the firm for the future. In planning jargon, these are called "intertemporal tradeoffs." These are the toughest decisions for any organization because they involve near-term pain for long-term gain, often after today's decision maker is long gone.

If senior leaders do not engage in future-making decisions, the organization risks being overtaken by the future. Even if decisions are made, there is no guarantee that they will be the correct ones. But if the decisions are the product of an honest, rigorous process designed to identify the best bets and best tradeoffs, then the organization has its greatest chance of success. This is the role of a formal future-making process. How planning can help senior managers make better future-making decisions is the subject of the next chapter.

In a Nutshell

▲ Organizations can make their futures by investing in new capabilities that will produce new services or products that might better meet future demand.

▲ Future making comes down to three fundamental precepts:

- First, make the best effort possible to understand what the future will demand;

- Then, determine what end states the organization must achieve to be successful in the future;

- Finally, act decisively to move towards the new end states.

▲ Planning without realistic resource constraints produces plans that are little more than unaffordable wish lists.

▲ The real building blocks of future making are decisions, which may or may not be made during a planning process and may or may not be embedded in a plan.

▲ If an organization's future-making decisions are the product of an honest, rigorous process designed to identify the best bets and best tradeoffs, then the organization has its greatest chance of success.

Notes

1 Andrew S. Grove, *Only the Paranoid Survive: How to Exploit the Crisis Points that Challenge Every Company* (New York: Doubleday, 1996), 89.

2 Ibid., 96–97.

3 Ibid., 132.

4 Michael Goold and John J. Quinn, *Strategic Control: Establishing Milestones for Long-Term Performance* (Reading, MA: Addison-Wesley Publishing Co., 1993), 7.

5 Thomas A. Stewart, "Did You Ever Have to Make Up Your Mind?" *Harvard Business Review* (January 2006), 12.

6 Gary Hamel, "Strategy as Revolution," *Harvard Business Review* (July–August 1996), 74.

2

Redefining the Role of
Planning, Planners, and Plans

FROM ITS HEYDAY IN THE 1960S AND 1970S, planning, especially when it's called strategic planning, has fallen on tough days. Firms and corporations in the private sector have sharply reduced their planning staffs. General Electric, once the poster child for formalized planning, essentially scrapped planning, fired the planners, and redefined the "GE way" in the 1980s and 1990s as building a "Boundaryless Learning Culture" and committed, admittedly in a "bit unbalanced" way, to its Six Sigma quality initiative.[1] Former Southwest Airlines CEO and now business icon Herb Kelleher could not have been more definite:

> We don't do strategic planning. It's a waste of time. You can spend three months coming up with something, and then you have to get buy-in from the other leadership. By the time you sell it to the board, things could have changed. Then you need to un-sell it to everyone before you can react. We don't do navel gazing. You miss opportunities when you're off thinking.[2]

Henry Mintzberg chronicled this decline in his seminal work, *The Rise and Fall of Strategic Planning*. His detailed, often acerbic, deconstruction of the discipline essentially hoists planning on its own petard by repeatedly underscoring the gap between planners' words and planners' deeds. For Mintzberg, strategic planning has become an oxymoron, and can be rescued only by limiting it to the implementation of strategies made by other means.[3]

There is no doubt that both those who have written about planning and those who have practiced it have suffered from Planner's Overreach, a disease that causes its victims to habitually promise more than they can possibly deliver. Planners have certainly provided plenty of ammunition for their detractors. I maintain, however, that organizations can and should plan for the future, but planning is not enough. To make it worthwhile, it must extend to future making, and that planners and planning can help senior management to become more future-oriented.

Redefining Planning as Organizational Future Making

Much organizational future making takes place informally—crises emerge, the CEO huddles with top management, and decisions are made that have strategic implications for the organization. This is a fact of life. An organization's *actual* strategy—what it does and doesn't do—is only revealed by its behavior over time. Relying on the daily "seat-of-the-pants" decisions of senior management, even when led by the legendary Herb Kelleher, usually leads to strategic choices that tend to be ad hoc, episodic, often uninformed, and too tightly tied to the present. Organizational future making is too important to be left *entirely* to informal processes. Planning, from this perspective, is future making done formally. It is the formal process by which an organization takes actions today to prepare to meet the future demand for goods, services, or capabilities.

Most definitions of planning don't include the words "takes action." But this book is about making your organization's future, not planning as an end in itself. The measure of success for planning is whether the organization takes steps to carry out its decisions or to implement its plan. Planning is the formal side of organizational future making. There are four principal future-making planning functions:

▲ **Define Future Demand.** You can't prepare for the future unless you define what you are preparing for. The planning horizon—

from 15 to 20 years for the Defense Department to 18 months for IT companies to 8 weeks (seemingly) for dot-com startups—depends on the nature of the business. How much uncertainty, as well as the amount of hedging required to deal with it, will also vary. The articulation of future demand should be the front end of all planning processes.

▲ **Set Strategic Directions.** The planning process can support the CEO by identifying the strategic choices facing an organization—the key decisions on what to do and what not to do—but it is the CEO and his top management that make the decision and establish strategic vectors for the organization. To cope with uncertainty, organizations need a clear sense of both who they are and where they are going. In other words, organizations need *identity* and *direction,* which are the fundamental building blocks of any strategic vision.

▲ **Convert Intent into Action.** What separates future making from future talking are the initial steps that an organization actually takes today in order to prepare for tomorrow. Planners who try to identify all the actions that eventually have to be taken (the end-to-end stream, so to speak) are overreaching. It is much more important to get approval of the initial actions that get the ball rolling. If the next decision point can be identified, so much the better. The strategic vision is implemented by the initial actions that can be incorporated in a strategic plan.

▲ **Follow Up.** Future making, by definition, involves making tough choices today that better position the organization to meet future demand. Accountability is critical. Planning without follow-up results in planning that produces no change, no future making. Strategic visions and plans are usually incomplete—no organization makes all its strategic decisions at one time, but follow up has to be systematic and complete. If decisions aren't implemented, the future doesn't get made.

Redefining planning as formalized future making provides clarity and focus. It is a formal process, although future-making decisions are also made informally. It focuses on future demand, not today's demand. And the bottom line for future-making planning is not what we think we should do to prepare to meet future demand, but what we actually do.

Redefining the Role of the Planner

The job of senior management is providing decisive, visionary leadership that enables their organization to cope with change and uncertainty. The leadership challenge, however, has intensified in this information era where everybody increasingly knows everything. A planner empowered to ask the tough questions of both the senior management's strategy—Is this going to make our organization's future?—and the leadership team itself—Is this how you want to be remembered?—can help those at the top provide coherent, purposive, value-centered leadership. For this to work effectively, the planner must earn and keep the CEO's trust and tolerance even as the planner is, in effect, telling his boss that he or she doesn't have any clothes on.

Planning is a staff function, not a line function. The planner has no direct authority—he does not make decisions for the organization, but facilitates decision making by the organization. Before there were organizations, there were "advisers" whose product (that is, advice) could be useful but was never necessary to those who received it. In fact, planners should read Herbert Goldhamer's classic treatise, *The Adviser,* on the trials and tribulations of advisers throughout history.[4] It will both remind them how powerless they really are but also how influential they can be. The key to the latter, of course, is always remembering the former.

▲ **Most definitions of planning don't include the words "takes action." But this book is about making your organization's future, not planning as an end in itself.**

Planners may have no rights, but they do have roles and responsibilities. In most instances, the planner's role is a facilitating one—she is not directly responsible for organizational learning, but she helps

Figure 2-1. The Future-Making Roles of the Planner

A planner empowered to ask the tough questions of both the senior management's strategy and the leadership team itself can help those at the top provide coherent, purposive, value-centered leadership.

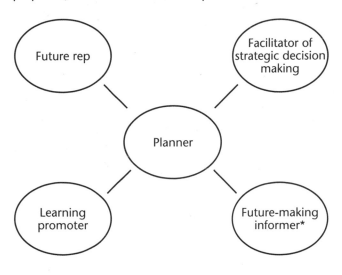

* The CEO is an organization's future-making cop, but the follow up function is so important that the planner must do anything in his or her power to get the CEO to act as the Enforcer-in-Chief.

the organization learn new things. The planner may be told to do many things—write speeches, conduct off-sites, prepare plans, and so on—but, as portrayed in Figure 2-1, she is critical to organizational future making in four primary roles: the Future Rep, the Learning Promoter, the Facilitator of Strategic Decision Making, and the Future-Making Informer.

Representing the Future

An organization can't make its own future without being future oriented. The long-range survival of any organization depends on how well it meets the future demand for its services, products, or capabilities. The CEO who wants to build an organization that lasts must give the future a seat at the table. He needs an advocate for the future, someone whose career depends on how well he informs senior leadership of the decisions its members must make for future success.

Most everybody in the company, including the CEO, is usually invested in the present. This is not surprising because meeting current demand is essential to organizational survival. No point thinking about tomorrow if you're going belly up today. Organizational future making is easiest when the organization is successful today. All too often, however, today's success breeds complacency about what will succeed tomorrow. Assigning those with current responsibilities the additional role of representing the future is asking them to behave unnaturally—that is, to dispassionately look at the very things that brought both the organization and themselves the success they enjoy today.

Organizations need a Future Rep who is not invested in today's way of doing business. Her view of future demand is much less likely to be influenced or shaped by today's way of meeting current demand. The Future Rep's most fundamental responsibility is to identify the future demand for an organization's capabilities, products, or services, and then to articulate that future demand at the various organizational tables.

Ask many planners, particularly if they are called "strategic planners," what their job is and they'll say it is to build plans for the organization's future. This is, perhaps, the most egregious case of Planner's Overreach. A plan, in its essence, represents the actions *on the supply side* that an organization will take to position itself to meet the future demand for its services or products. Planners who believe they are responsible for both advocating future demand *and* advocating how the organization will meet that demand are claiming too much for themselves and asking too little from their bosses. The result—plans with no beef.

Only the CEO and his senior line management team can decide what the organization will supply in the future. And since most companies have constrained resources, a decision to supply something new in the future must be accompanied by a decision on what the company will stop doing today. Without this latter decision, it is likely that not enough resources will be available to invest in building the future capability. Planners, by definition, can't make any decisions about what to give up because they have no line responsibilities. And senior managers don't like deciding what to stop doing because these decisions directly affect those currently engaged in those activities. It is particularly difficult when those decisions are formally ensconced in a "plan" that makes it obvious to all whose ox got gored as the firm positions itself for the future.

Tough decisions at the top on the trade-offs between current supply and future supply are the *sine qua non* of successful organizational future making. A future making or planning process that produces only new-start decisions is not a serious one. There is no free lunch. The planner's role as Future Rep must be evaluated against the stop-now standard—is his portrayal of the future compelling enough to persuade the organization to stop doing something today?

The convincing articulation of future demand is threatening enough, because somebody has to start paying the price for preparing to meet future demand. If the planner also straps on the job of advocating how to meet that demand, he has identified precisely who will pay the price for change. And the bill payer for change now knows who his enemy is. Better a live Future Rep than a dead (overreaching) planner. Stay on message—represent the future, but only on the demand side.

Promoting Organizational Learning

Organizational future making is predicated on organizational learning—organizations don't change their behavior unless they have learned something new. The Future Rep's work is in vain unless the organization "learns it" and acts on it. The organization that doesn't learn stays with what it knows—a recipe for disaster in today's business climate.

Organizations, however, do not literally learn; people occupying positions in organizations learn or, more often, fail to learn. Arie P. De Geus, the path-breaking planner for Royal Dutch Shell, argues strongly that planning should be seen as learning and observes tartly that "the only relevant learning in a company is the learning done by those people who have the power to act."[5] This is the bottom line—an organization hasn't really learned anything about the future unless it acts on that knowledge.

But people throughout any organization learn. The issue is how to bring that knowledge to bear on those who make decisions on behalf of the organization. Former CEO and now Chairman of Intel Andrew Grove stresses the important role that the "helpful Cassandras" on the company's front line can play in sensing when a company is about to be overcome by fundamental shifts in the demand for its products.[6] Noting that snow on the mountain top always starts melting at the periphery, Grove insists that the successful CEO must always keep his ear to the ground, stay open to new information and never, never kill the messenger. How many CEOs do you know like that?

▲ **This is the bottom line—an organization hasn't really learned anything about the future unless it acts on that knowledge.**

Gary Hamel with his "tyranny of experience" has it right—those at the top of successful organizations are the ones most invested in today's way of doing business. They fought their way to the top by doing what works today.* These are not shy, retiring folks. They are the most prone to intellectual arrogance: "It's my idea; it must be right." After all, they have the track record to prove it. Counting on those at the top to promote organizational learning is likely to fail. They neither have the time (somebody has to run the company) nor the inclination (nothing succeeds like success) for it.

It is not enough for the planner to represent the future; he must also promote sufficient organizational learning about the future to

---

* Obviously, this characterization doesn't apply to those senior managers recently brought in from the outside or those who have survived an organization's or industry's "near death" experience." However, the challenge that so many organizations face today is coping with discontinuous change, when, by definition, what worked in the past won't work in the future. Organizations that bring in new leadership from the outside have already learned that lesson.

stimulate action. He must represent the future in a way that convinces senior management to take ownership of the need to change and then to take action. To foster successful organizational future making, the planner must recognize that his Future Rep role is not just truth telling. Emperors don't like to be told they are wearing no clothes. The planner's role as Learning Promoter shapes how he functions as Future Rep.

Leaders learn in different ways. What works with one doesn't work with another. They differ greatly in their tolerance for dissent or openness to new things. Planners too often become purists in their Future Rep role, forgetting that it is not their understanding of future demand that matters, but their bosses' understanding. Representing the future in a way that promotes organizational learning is far from straightforward. How well the planner plays his role as Learning Promoter, however, can determine how well the organization succeeds in future making—does it make the tough decisions that free up resources for investing in the future?

Facilitating Strategic Decision Making

Over the past two decades, I've advised, counseled, supported, assisted, or simply worked for many "principals." My experience is that small, reactive, instant decisions—"mini-decisions," so to speak—come easily to most members of the senior management team, but few possess a real willingness to take on tough problems and actually do something about them.

The military reputation of Ulysses S. Grant has enjoyed a recent renaissance. Not only did he win all of his campaigns, but, in a record unmatched by any other American general, his troops forced the surrender of three enemy armies. In a quite perceptive book review, Princeton historian James M. McPherson stresses Grant's ability "to make a decision and stick to it":

> Grant proved his physical courage under fire many times in the Mexican War as well as in the Civil War. So did many others. But as Grant noted, the willingness to take responsibility and to make

decisions—or what Grant called "moral courage"—was much rarer. It is a readiness to take risks, and to accept the possibility of failure, for without the risk of failure there is no chance of success. Fear of failure causes paralysis of will and evasion of action.[7]

Recently, the how-to mavens (of which I am one) have stressed the role of corporate leaders as community builders, creating visionary or learning or quality companies. For me, the leader of an organization, firm, or company is the one who takes on the tough problems, makes a decision on what should be done, and then makes sure it gets done.

The planner can help identify the strategic choices facing a firm; the senior managers need to be involved in setting new vectors; but it is usually the CEO who drives the decision on which direction to go and which direction *not* to go. Deciding what to give up in order to move in another direction is tough and requires the "moral courage" of Ulysses S. Grant or the "guts" of Jack Welch. Former Intel CEO Andrew Grove questioned whether anyone in an organization can be motivated to succeed by an indecisive boss and "his direction *du jour*" and then commented:

> I can't help but wonder why leaders are so often hesitant to lead. I guess it takes a lot of conviction and trusting your gut to get ahead of your peers, your staff and your employees while they are still squabbling about which path to take, and set an unhesitating, unequivocal course whose rightness or wrongness will not be known for years. Such a decision really tests the mettle of the leader.[8]

Making tough decisions and then sticking to them is what leadership is all about, no matter what the line of business.

The planner's role as Strategic Decision Making Facilitator must begin with self-restraint. Planners have lots of ideas about the future and want to define a comprehensive strategic vision. One's appetite for new starts should always be suppressed by knowing the price you have to pay for new initiatives. If you only say what you really mean, you say less. The same is true for planning—serious plans incorporate strategic decisions on what to do and what not to do. Effective,

▲ ━━━━━━━━━━━━━━━━━━━━━━━━━━━━━━━━

Future Making vs. Future Talking

Planning processes that produce only new-start decisions usually lose credibility and relevance. A "wish list" of new initiatives that comprises an organization's strategic vision is only as good as the list of stop-now actions backstopping it. Otherwise, the strategic intent expressed in the vision is not serious. It's talking about the future, not future making.

During a 1996 visioning summit, the Air Force's senior civilian and military leadership set forth an ambitious vision of how it would change to meet the nation's growing demand for air and space power. But the question of how to pay for these changes (the Air Force's planners estimated at the time that the price tag for implementing these strategic choices would be five to eight billion dollars per year for 20 years) was deferred until later. The stop-now decisions were to be handled separately in a "divestiture drill" as part of the implementation process. Despite three separate attempts, no decisions were made on what to stop doing. The subsequent long-range plan that implemented the strategic intent expressed at the summit had little impact because it was unaffordable. ▲

━━━━━━━━━━━━━━━━━━━━━━━━━━━━━━━━

decision-oriented plans are crisp and short. In fact, although it's an untested hypothesis, there may be an inverse relationship between a plan's length and its relevance.

In this book, I argue that CEOs must redefine planning and the role of planners to help them make their organizations' futures. In "Stop Making Plans; Start Making Decisions" Michael C. Mankins and Richard Steele argue forcefully that "many executives have grown skeptical of strategic planning" because their research suggests that strategic planning processes are "often a barrier to good decision making:"

The failure of most strategic planning is due to two factors: It is typically an annual process, and it is most often focused on individual business units. As such the process is completely at odds with the way executives actually make important strategy decisions. . . .They make the decisions that really shape their company's strategy and determine its future* —decisions about mergers and acquisitions, product launches, corporate restructurings, and the like—outside the planning process, typically in an ad hoc fashion, without rigorous analysis or productive debate. Critical decisions are made incorrectly or not at all.[9]

Exactly right, I say, and that's why we need to redefine strategic planning and the role of the planner. And that turns out to be Mankins and Steele's position as well. Noting that "strategic planning can't have impact if it doesn't drive decision making," they call for "decision-focused strategic planning" that replaces "traditional" planning (with its annual process and its focus on business units) with "continuous, decision-oriented planning:"

> Once the company as a whole has identified its most important strategic priorities (typically in an annual strategy update), executive committee dialogues . . . are set up to reach decisions on as many issues as possible. . . . task forces are established to prepare the strategic and financial information that's needed to uncover and evaluate strategy alternatives for each issue. . . .Once a decision has been reached, the budgets and capital plans for the affected business units are updated to reflect the selected option. Consequently, the strategic-planning process and the capital and budgeting processes are integrated. . . . **The results: a concrete plan for addressing each key issue; for each business unit, a continuously updated budget and capital plan that is linked directly to the resolution of critical strategic issues; and more, faster, better decisions per year.**[10]

Although their recommended approach seems to contradict the injunction to "stop making plans" and still embraces the notion of "strategic-planning process," I agree that this is a good way to implement decisions made at the "annual strategy update." After all, "iden-

---

* As a personal aside, this is the first of several instances in which I've learned of the risks involved in letting my manuscript for Future Making sit unpublished for five years. "Future determining" is awfully close to "future making." I may preach follow through and execution, but in this instance, I failed to heed my own advice.

tifying its most important strategic priorities" requires big strategic choices by the CEO and his senior team. These decisions about a company's strategic direction are too important not to be captured in an authoritative document and disseminated widely throughout the company. If, as Mankins and Steele imply, the decisions made at the "annual strategic update," are "limited" (I use the term advisedly, because most strategic planning off-sites don't even do this) to identifying strategic priorities and establishing a firm's annual agenda for strategic decision making, this document might be called the Annual Strategic Guidance statement. My experience, however, with guidance documents, (in the Department of Defense, for example, defense planning guidance, strategic planning guidance, and joint programming guidance, to name a few) suggests that it's pretty easy to ignore "guidance." That's why, as I'll argue shortly, what is widely known as a company's "strategic planning off-site" (which Mankins and Steele call an annual strategic update) should include decisions about the *initial actions* a company should take in pursuing their strategic vectors and that these decisions should be incorporated in a company (not a business unit) "strategic plan."

A more fundamental counter to my (and Mankins' and Steele's) contention that strategic planning can still matter is posed by Jeffrey Pfeffer and Robert I. Sutton in *Hard Facts, Dangerous Half-Truths & Total Nonsense*. After suggesting that eBay CEO Meg Whitman attributes much of her company's success "to the fact that the company spends less time on strategic analysis and more time trying and tweaking things that seem like they might work, and learning along the way," Pfeffer and Sutton conclude:

> The idea is a simple one, but one that is not often implemented and is belied by the focus on planning and strategic focus: learn as you go. As Andy Grove, former CEO of Intel, said in an interview with Clayton Christensen of the Harvard Business School, "None of us has a real understanding of where we are heading. I don't. I have sense about it...but decisions don't wait. Investment decisions or personnel decisions and prioritization don't wait for the picture to be clarified. You have to make them when you have

to make them. So you take your shots and clean up the bad ones later.[11]

While initially chagrinned at having my favorite former-CEO-now-strategy-guru in opposition to my belief that planning *can* (not *does*) matter, I believe that Grove is really saying that when a decision has be made, you have to make it, regardless of how much analysis you have done or whether it fits in the planning cycle. No one disagrees with this or with the statement that you should learn as you go, because implementing decisions blindly and without feedback mechanisms courts disaster. But so does relying on ad hoc decisions made by CEOs who are prone to being too invested in how they do business today and are in a state of denial about what the future might bring.

Policing Organizational Future Making

Making the future begins with steps taken today by operational units over whom the planner has no control. Who can ensure that the organization sticks to the decisions it makes? Only the CEO and his most senior line managers. Critical to successful future making is follow up—making sure that decisions made are implemented.

Follow up is grubby, often mean-spirited work, because it implicitly questions the good faith of one's subordinates by asking if they did what they were told to do. Even decisive CEOs prefer the new business of making more new-start decisions than the old business of follow up. It is the failure to follow up on future-making decisions, however, that undermines so many planning processes. Decisions get made; no one is held accountable for implementation failures; and organizations drift into the future rather than try to make it.

Discipline and accountability are not descriptors usually associated with strategic planning. But they are absolutely critical for *serious* future making. Failure to carry out future-making decisions must be treated as transgressions of corporate trust. CEOs should take it personally when their decisions, particularly their big strategic choices on how their company will prepare for the future, are not being executed. After all, their time is too valuable to be wasted in making meaningless decisions.

The planner cannot play the role of Future-Making Enforcer, because he has no authority or line responsibilities. It's the senior team, led by the CEO, that must act as the cop, the jury, and the judge. However, the planner does have a role, as it often falls on him or her to act as "the snitch" for the "legal authorities." This is unpleasant duty. No one likes being a tattle-tale (see Figure 2-1). No one likes confronting valued colleagues. This is the dark side of future making.

▲ **Discipline and accountability are not descriptors usually associated with strategic planning. But they are absolutely critical for serious future making.**

Accountability is at the heart of serious future making. Future-making decisions must be implemented. Otherwise, why make them? Policing the future-making process is rough work, but essential. It separates the future talkers from the future walkers. It's about sticking to the decisions you've made.

The Planning Process— Whatever Works for the Senior Team

The scarcest commodity in any organization is senior management time—there aren't enough hours in the day to do everything that needs to be done. Globalization, the Information Age and the Internet all contribute to a more uncertain, more competitive world. The pressure on senior leadership to meet current demand is relentless. It makes it really hard to raise one's sights towards future demand.

A CEO can't do serious future making unless he spends time at it. Andrew Grove underscores that point:

One more word about your time: if you're in a leadership position, how you spend your time has enormous symbolic value. It will communicate what's important or what isn't far more powerfully than all the speeches you can give.

Strategic change doesn't just start at the top. It starts with your calendar.[12]

A planning process that doesn't have CEO involvement is a waste of time for the organization. But one that does have CEO involvement is a double-barreled commitment. It tells the organization's senior stakeholders, both inside and outside the organization, that future making is important. It also commits the CEO to setting aside time for formal future making. And it is this time that enables the planner in all of his roles—Future Rep, Learning Promoter, Facilitator of Strategic Decision Making, and the Future-Making Informer.

There is no one right way to organize this process. The common ingredient is senior management time dedicated to future making. Perhaps the most inclusive or collective planning function is Defining Future Demand—a wider net (at senior levels) catches more ideas, more insight, more buy-in. Probably the least inclusive function is Follow-Up, which may best be done in a series of one-on-one meetings between the CEO and his top managers. The people involved in Setting Strategic Direction could be as broad as those who Defined Future Demand, but they could be limited to those who possess real decision-making authority in the organization. Similarly, the organizational unit that approves the set of Initial Actions could be limited to the key actors in the resource allocation process. The only "must-have" design principle: CEO involvement in all four functions.

Future making must be a deliberate process for an organization. It is not enough to "keep the future in mind" as one goes about the daily grind. It's also critical for the senior management team to take a time-out from today's in-basket and make themselves think about the future. Empowering the planner with a formal planning process gives him opportunities—off-sites, planning sessions, vision summits, and so on—to promote organizational learning, facilitate strategic decision making, and police future making. An organization can't successfully make its future unless it makes time for future making. Without a formal planning process, there are simply not enough opportunities to get everybody's head, but especially the CEO's, into the future.

Figure 2-2. The Planning Hierarchy and Future-Making Planning Functions

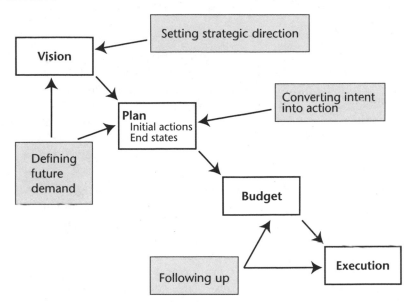

There is no one right way to organize the future-making planning process. The only "must-have" design principle is CEO involvement in all four functions.

Planning Products—A Vision and a Plan

As portrayed in Figure 2-2, an organization's vision document is at the top of the planning hierarchy. While most strategic visions convey a sense of "who we are" as an organization, a future-making vision must have two elements—a succinct characterization of future demand (what the organization is preparing to meet) and the changes in direction that the organization will make to meet that demand. Serious future making is about committing to change and then making change happen. The vision document, from this perspective, is a statement for the record—this is what the future holds and this is how the organization will prepare for it. It sets the bar for future making by providing a standard for assessing how well an organization's actions live up to its words.

In Their Own Words: CEOs as Strategic Operators

John Chambers, CEO of Cisco Systems Inc.:[1]

On defining his job: "having responsibility for setting the strategy at Cisco . . . [is] one of the top three things I do. The second thing that I do is recruit and develop and retain the leadership team that is going to be able to implement that strategy. The third thing that I do is really focus on what culture we want here at Cisco . . . .The leader must walk his or her talk. So if you say customer success is most important, I still listen to every critical account in the world every night."

On follow-up: "This is where the Web-based architecture is so key, because I can see an automatic roll-up [summary] of customer satisfaction very quickly any time I want. I can see an automatic roll-up of every order around the world and explode that down, not just by key geographies . . . (but) by country or by city or by key customer, even to an individual sales rep. . . . And then we, I, listen to constructive criticism . . . definitely a lot more than you do [to] compliments."

Lawrence J. Ellison, CEO, Oracle Corporation:[2]

On his vision to create the first-ever "e-business suite": "We have a chance to pass Microsoft and become the No. 1 software company. If I said that two years ago, I would have been sedated and locked up. But now we're the Internet, and they are not."

On the impact of moving everything to one central database: "When you're an e-business, everything is mediated by computers. All the individuality is bled out of the system and replaced by standards. People don't run their own show any more." As Business Week commented, "That makes it easy for executives to get a comprehensive view of operations and spot trouble before it gets out of hand."

1 Scott Thurm, "How to Drive an Express Train," *Wall Street Journal,* June 2, 2000.
2 Steve Hamm, "Oracle: Why It's Cool Again," *Business Week,* May 8, 2000. ▲

A future-making vision document expresses strategic intent; the plan converts intent into action. The plan implements the vision by adding specificity, both to the articulation of future demand and the definition of the End States that comprise the destination. The End States are the desired results—in other words, the objectives to be accomplished in a certain time phase. End States are the goal line, which must be crossed in order to score. No goal line; no scoring. Identifying the End States brings accountability to planning.

Every journey begins with a single step. Planners overreach when they attempt to identify all the steps necessary to reach the End States. End-to-end plans are wrong the moment they are produced, because the world will have changed by the time intermediate steps are reached. What is critical is to identify the Initial Actions, the concrete steps to take now to better position the organization for the future. The strategic vision provides the sense of direction; the plan identifies what steps to take first and what the last step looks like.

Planners used to debate whether it was planning or the plan that was important. The fact of the matter is that you can't have one without the other. A process that produces no products is a waste of time. A product can't be made without a process. When an organization commits to a formal planning process and formal planning products, it is making time for future making.

Visioning and planning can generate decisions about what to do to prepare for the future; ensuring that actions are actually taken to prepare for the future is the bottom line. That's why follow up is so critical, for without it, planning becomes a self-licking ice cream cone. But if no meaningful decisions are made as the vision and plan are produced, there is nothing to follow up. Future making requires both decisions and actions.

The CEO as Strategic Operator

Organizational future making occurs in both informal and formal processes. Daily decisions sometimes have long-term, strategic impacts that are frequently not anticipated or intended by those making the decisions. During the planning cycle, organizations formally address the strategic choices facing them. Future-making decisions, both those taken formally and informally, have intended and unintended consequences; sometimes the resulting actions serve the purposes of the decision makers—sometimes they don't. It is the totality of the actions that a firm takes (or doesn't take) that determines how well it prepares to meet future demand. It's the actions that count, not how the decisions were made that led to the actions.

How strategically an organization behaves can only be determined over time. Is there a purpose or pattern to its actions? Has the company made tough decisions yesterday that better prepared it to meet today's demand? Is today's success the residue of luck or skill? Not all actions will fit the pattern; no one has perfect foresight and compromises are often necessary—but actions speak louder than words. Some organizations make their futures; others let the future happen to them.

All senior managers must be operators, that is, decision makers who are tactically adept and excel at meeting current demand. Under constant pressure from multiple sources, the top jobs are "in-box" jobs that demand an almost Pavlovian response to a stream of inputs from inside and outside the organization. Successfully meeting current demand is more than a full-time job, making it difficult for any CEO to keep an eye on the future when today's crises demand attention. But how well the CEO prepares for the future may be his most important job. That's particularly true for "built-to-last" companies that fully intend to be permanent players. But even "built-to-flip" organizations must look like they have "made futures."

It is the planner's job to help his CEO act as a Strategic Operator. He represents future demand. The planner can help the CEO understand the future implications of the decisions he makes. The future is the planner's domain. How effectively he articulates future demand will affect how strategically the CEO operates. Making the future seem real today is part of convincing the CEO and his senior management team to make tough decisions today. How the Planner does this is the subject of the next chapter.

In a Nutshell

▲ Planning is future making done formally. It is the formal process by which an organization takes actions today to prepare to meet the future demand for its goods and services.

▲ Future-making planning has four principal functions:
  • Defining the future demand for an organization's products, services, or capabilities;
  • Setting the strategic direction for how the organization will position itself to meet that future demand;
  • Converting that strategic intent into action by identifying the end states to be achieved and the initial steps to be taken;
  • Following up to make sure that future-making decisions are implemented.

▲ Senior managers are usually too invested in the present to look dispassionately at future demand. All too often, today's success breeds complacency about what will succeed tomorrow.

▲ Empowering a planner gives the future a seat at the table. His most fundamental responsibility is to identify the future demand and then advocate for that future demand.

▲ The planner must promote sufficient organizational learning about the future to convince senior management to "take ownership" of the need to change.

▲ A planner can help identify the strategic choices facing a firm, but it is usually the CEO who drives the decision on which direction to go and which direction not to go.

▲ It is the failure to follow up on future-making decisions that undermines so many planning processes. Discipline and accountability are critical to serious future making. Effective follow up separates the future makers from the future talkers.

▲ There is no one right way to organize planning. The critical ingredient is senior management time dedicated to future making. A planning process that doesn't have CEO involvement is a waste of time.

Notes

1 John F. Welch, "A Learning Company and its Quest for Six Sigma" (Presentation at the General Electric Company 1999 Annual Meeting, Cleveland, OH, April 21, 1999).

2 Jeffrey Pfeffer and Robert I. Sutton, *Hard Facts, Dangerous Half-Truths & Total Nonsense: Profiting from Evidence-Based Management* (Boston, MA: Harvard Business School Press, 2006), 155. Original citation: Darrin Earl, "Kelleher Visits McComb," *Texas Business Weekly* (February 5, 2003).

3 Henry Mintzberg, *The Rise and Fall of Strategic Planning: Reconceiving Roles for Planning, Plans, Planners* (New York: The Free Press, 1994).

4 Herbert Goldhamer, *The Adviser* (New York: Elsevier, 1978).

5 Arie P. De Geus, "Planning as Learning," *Harvard Business Review* (March-April 1988), 71.

6 Andrew S. Grove, *Only the Paranoid Survive: How to Exploit the Crisis Points that Challenge Every Company* (New York: Doubleday, 1996), 108-120.

7 James M. McPherson, "The Riddle of the Victor," *New Republic* (February 21, 2000), 43-44.

8 Grove, *Only the Paranoid Survive,* 142-143.

9 Michael C. Mankins and Richard Steele, "Stop Making Plans; Start Making Decisions," *Harvard Business Review* (January 2006), 78.

10 Ibid., 80, 83.

11 Pfeffer and Sutton, *Hard Facts, Dangerous Half-Truths,* 155.

12 Grove, *Only the Paranoid Survive,* 146.

3

Defining Future Demand

Organizational future making begins with a dispassionate effort to define the future demand for an organization's products, services, or capabilities. In this textbook-like formulation, this assertion is a no-brainer. Of course, an organization that wants to prosper in the future should prepare to meet future demand, not today's demand—after all, in the future, today's demand is history.

Gary Hamel and Liisa Valikangas argue convincingly that companies seeking to survive turbulent times must be "strategically resilient." That is, they must have the "ability to dynamically reinvent business models and strategies as circumstances change," and they must be "as efficient at renewal as they are at producing today's goods and services":

> The goal [for "zero trauma" resilience] is a strategy that is forever morphing, forever conforming itself to emerging opportunities and incipient trends. The goal is an organization that is constantly making its future* rather than defending its past. The goal is a company where revolutionary change happens in lightning-quick, evolutionary steps—with no calamitous surprises, no convulsive reorganizations, no colossal write-offs, and no indiscriminate, across-the-board layoffs.[1]

---

* In this instance of the risks I took in letting *Future Making* go unpublished for a number of years, Hamel and Valikangas actually use the words "making" and "future." Good thing for me they were using "resilient organization" as their paradigm.

On Denial

by Gary Hamel and Liisa Valikangas

"Every business is successful until it's not. What's amazing is how often top management is surprised when 'not' happens. This astonishment, this belated recognition of dramatically changed circumstances, virtually guarantees that the work of renewal will be significantly, perhaps dangerously, postponed."

After noting that IT investments had tripled, from 19 percent to 59 percent, in its share of U.S. corporate capital budgets, Hamel and Valikangas wrote "anyone looking at the data in 2000 should have been asking, Will capital spending keep growing at a double-digit pace? And is it likely that IT spending will continue to grow so fast. Logically, the answer to both questions had to be no. Things that can't go on forever usually don't."

"The fact that serious performance shortfalls so often come as a surprise suggests that executives frequently take refuge in denial. Greg Blonder, former chief technical adviser at AT&T, admitted as much in a November 2002 Barron's article: 'In the early 1990s, AT&T management argued internally that the steady upward curve of Internet usage would somehow collapse. The idea that it might actually overshadow traditional telephone service was simply unthinkable. But the trend could not be stopped—or even slowed—by wishful thinking and clever marketing. One by one, the props that held up the long-distance business collapsed.' For AT&T, as for many other companies, the future was less unknowable than it was unthinkable, less inscrutable than unpalatable."

Defining and meeting future demand, not just better execution in meeting today's demand, is critical to the long-term survival of any company.

But the obstacles to defining future demand, particularly during an era of rapid, discontinuous change, are huge and have both psychological and cognitive dimensions. Taking a dispassionate, coldly objective perspective in assessing whether today's way of doing business will fit tomorrow's demand requires self-discipline and a capacity to distance oneself emotionally. Former PepsiCo Chairman and CEO Roger A. Enrico insisted that "every single day, you have to think and act as if your business is expendable. I don't think there is any such thing as sustainable competitive advantage anymore."[2] Maintaining that level of dispassion is beyond most of us.

To repeat an earlier point, an organization's decisions are made by the men and women holding the top jobs in the organization. The all too human tendency is to look at the future through rose-colored glasses and make the future safe for today's way of doing business. Richard McGinn, former Chairman and CEO of Lucent Technologies, was summarily fired in October 2000 because of Lucent's repeated failures to meet his earnings projections. Corporate insiders reported that several members of his senior management team had tried to convince him that his projections were unrealistic (because new products weren't ready and the sale of older ones would decline), but he "absolutely rejected" the advice: "He said the market is growing and there's absolutely no reason why we can't grow. He was in total denial."[3] Denial, as Mark Twain said, ain't just a river in Egypt.

As difficult as the psychological barriers to defining future demand may be, the cognitive barriers may be even harder. There are those who argue that the future is fundamentally unknowable, making any effort to define future demand an exercise in futility. Let's take a closer look at this obstacle to organizational future making before proceeding further.

How Chaotic and Unknowable Is the Future?

The "new science" of chaos theory and complexity provides a scientific foundation for dismissing the utility of planning in general and future making in particular.[4] Forecasting has always been difficult, but the profounder understanding of how nonlinear systems behave makes the future unknowable, goes this argument. Plans are therefore useless because there is no reliable way to link actions taken in the present with desired end states in the future. There is no point in future making when no one knows what will work. The solution of the complexity mavens: create a community in which all of the members of the organization share a vision of a desired future and let them "self-organize" to cope with the challenges as they emerge (in the Pentagon, for example, they say distributed units would "self-synchronize" around the commander's intent).

This is not a trivial argument. Surviving, much less succeeding, in this era of increasingly rapid change and uncertainty seems harder and harder, and many firms have indeed disbanded their planning shops and scrapped formal strategic planning. But is "Ready? Fire!" really the answer? Doesn't it help to aim? It does. And it helps to have a target to aim at.

There is a breathless quality to much of the literature grounded in chaos and complexity. For example, Darryl R. Conner paints an intimidating picture:

> The world is inundated with disruptions: unforeseen dangers, unanticipated opportunities, unmet expectations, alarming new statistics, startling twists of fate, shocking innovations, unheralded improvements, unrealistic requirements, overwhelming demands, contradictory directives, staggering liabilities, astonishing results, sudden strokes of luck, and more. At every turn, there is something that we didn't see coming.[5]

Of course, there are big surprises—the sudden collapse of the Soviet Union, for example. But in the aftermath of that collapse, many correctly predicted that the struggling Russia that emerged would have a long and difficult time ahead. Companies thinking about betting their future on the prospect of an enormous pent-up demand for consumer goods would want this input.

Many things about the future are, to a great extent, knowable: demographics rarely mislead; nor do environmental trends. Most technological trends come slower (usually) or faster than initially believed, but they do come. Analysis may not tell you precisely what the future demand for your products or capabilities will be, but it can often identify what it won't be. Understanding the implications of what is knowable about the future can help any organization make its future. And, as Philip Evans and Thomas S. Wurster observed, organizations don't have any choice; they have to think about the future:

> "Chaos" may be a powerful paradigm for economists, genuinely high-tech businesses, and venture capitalists who are in the business of making bets. But corporations are instruments for deploying resources strategically, with the advantages inherent in large-scale organization. Without understanding the real pervasiveness of uncertainty, it seemed to us *essential* that strategy be based on what is knowable rather than what is unknowable. Embracing chaos is an admission of defeat.[6]

Of course, there are always unintended consequences to our actions. But there are also *intended* consequences. I believe in making things happen.

A Planner at the Table Can Help Future Making

Planners and *plans:* the very words have connotations—deliberate, methodical, comprehensive, systematic, long-range—that seem out of step in today's fast-paced economy. When the Air Force set up its new planning office in late 1995, the newly appointed special assistant for long-range planning visited Microsoft to see how they did planning. He was dismayed to learn they didn't do any planning at all. Instead, their business strategy was to strike quickly to exploit emerging (and fleeting) market opportunities. One research director, in fact, expressed great pride in taking a product from conception to the market in six weeks. What's the role of the planner in this world?

The planning or time horizons associated with organizational future making depend on the nature of the business. Some industries, such as pharmaceuticals or aircraft, have seven to ten year development cycles, while others, for example, fashion or financial services, have cycles of less than a year. Few question the relevance of planning when the time horizons are long, because common sense suggests that the demand for products or capabilities could be different five or ten years from today. But how about much shorter product development cycles?

Anticipating the Future, as Practiced by Michael J. Critelli, Chairman and CEO, Pitney Bowes

As chairman and CEO I spend a large proportion of my time—about 25%—on strategy. Speculation about our future enters into every discussion with every investor, it factors into customers' decisions on investing in capital equipment, and potential employees pose questions about it when they're considering joining us.

Thinking strategically, of course, begins with making predictions about the future, and that means perceiving the direction in which things are changing. You have to start with the facts about trends. . . . But directional understanding is only the beginning; the real key is gauging the rate of change. Are we looking at slow growth, flat volumes, a gradual decline that we can live with, or acceleration into a faster decline? That's the question we wrestle with—because if the latter is the case, we're in danger of entering a death spiral and should take more drastic action to move into adjacent spaces.

My strategic responsibility to the company is to ensure that the thinking [about the future] is being done and that actions are taken as a result. Soon after becoming the chairman, I created a role reporting directly to me, focused on anticipating the future. The man I hired, Luis Jimenez (he is now our chief strategy officer), had headed the postal practice for consulting firm Arthur D. Little for 16 years and worked extensively on modeling the different components of the mail stream. We've also dedicated another full-time professional to looking at factors that could influence the future of mail, and we use techniques like scenario planning (as famously pioneered by Royal Dutch/Shell) to understand how they will evolve. We have a postal policy council of senior executives that convenes regularly to look at the data and ask, Is there anything new in the environment that could change our basic conclusions? We're constantly monitoring the landscape for changing conditions.

Future making is future making, no matter how short the time horizon. Any organization, company, or firm must ask whether there is a future demand for its products, services, or capabilities, and, depending on the answer, decide what to do. The senior managers, including the CEO, are usually too wedded, too invested in how the firm meets today's demand to be objective or dispassionate about whether their current products will be relevant in the future, whether that future is six months or six years away.

Ten years ago, Microsoft lived in a computing world dominated by PCs, and its operating system ruled. It focused on maintaining barriers to entry and doing more of what it already was doing, but faster, better, and cheaper. Microsoft did not anticipate the direction that computing would take as computing power, driven by Moore's Law, rapidly increased. On the other hand, Larry Ellison, Oracle's CEO, believed that computing would move to huge servers that would power the Internet and that networked computers would rule in place of individual PCs capable only of Web-surfing and e-mail. A Microsoft vice president commented at the time that "philosophically speaking, Larry [Ellison] has always been anti-personal computer. He was then, and he is today. His device is a replacement for the PC. We're not trying to do that. We firmly believe in the PC."[7] Microsoft, of course, has moved big time into Internet-based services, but its world view still remained PC-centric: when he introduced an operating system upgrade in February 2001, Chairman Bill Gates said, "People want to do more and more with their PCs. Windows XP builds on their dreams, taking the power and adaptability of the PC to a new level."[8] On the other hand, a former PC true believer who was getting out of the PC business, Mircon Electronics CEO Joel Kocher, said, "You'd have to be deaf, dumb, and blind not to see where things are going [the migration of computing from PCs to the Net]."[9] This wasn't an argument about future demand; this was a contest, in this case quite personal, over who had the right product.

Organizations produce things that meet demand. It's only human nature that the people at the top of successful organizations will be personally committed to their current products. Their projections of future demand will be biased by their unconscious desire

Betting on the Future

The struggle over whether PCs or huge servers would dominate the future of computing had many dimensions. As part of its effort to keep the PC at the center of the Internet, Microsoft reorganized its business structure three times in 18 months to push its new "Microsoft.Net" initiative, announced in June 2000. Microsoft CEO Steve Ballmer left little to the imagination about why: "Just as the Windows platform has powered the growth of the personal computer industry over the past 20 years, we are now well-positioned to create software and services that will power tomorrow's Internet and take advantage of significant opportunities in wireless, new devices, small business, games and TV."[1]

Microsoft also developed a product to compete with Oracle's network computer, an idea that Oracle CEO Larry Ellison had been pushing for a decade. Ellison's reaction was scathing: "Microsoft has four stages in stealing someone else's idea. First is 'This is incredibly stupid.' Then it's 'This is stupid, but there are interesting things about it.' Third is 'We have a version, and ours is better.' And the fourth is 'What are you talking about? We invented it.' That's what Bill calls innovation."[2]

At the same time that Microsoft countered Oracle's effort to provide a full suite of Internet-based applications, its flank was attacked by an old adversary, IBM. IBM threw big bucks, not to mention a thousand programmers, behind the Linux operating system, which it offered free over the Internet. IBM's decision to bet on Linux, which has become the open source alternative to Microsoft, is not just payback but its adaptation to fast, discontinuous change. As IBM's point man at the time and future CEO, Sam Palmisano observed: "The Internet has taught us all the importance of moving early, the advantage of being a first-mover. We want to be riding that Linux momentum at the front, not trailing it and defending the past. I.B.M. understands, believe me, what it means to be defending the past."[3]

---

1 Rebecca Buckman, "Microsoft Makes Changes to Focus on Internet, *Wall Street Journal* (August 10, 2000).

2 David Streitfeld, "For a Dead Idea, the 'Network Computer' is Downright Sprightly," *Washington Post* (June 11, 2000).

3 Steve Lohr, "A Mainstream Giant Goes Countercultural," *New York Times* (March 20, 2000). ▲

to make the future safe for their current products. Most CEOs will understand the need to make improvements or cut costs—this is the traditional Coke vs. Pepsi or Betty Crocker vs. Doughboy competition—but most will not see the possibility of having to produce something else entirely. Yet this is precisely what may be required in an era of rapid, discontinuous change when disruptive technologies redefine entire industries. It's the planner's job to ask the "what if" questions and make the "but, sir" interventions. But in order to do this when it counts, he or she has to have a seat at the table.

Representing the Future

Making room at the table for the planner is, in effect, giving the future a seat at the table. What does it mean to represent the future? If done effectively, it ensures that when an organization makes or doesn't make a decision, it understands the future implications of that decision or non-decision. But the role of Future Rep is not an easy one. Crying wolf too many times erodes a planner's credibility. Nor does senior management like being told they are wearing no clothes. This is politics with a small "p," but the planner must know how to play the game to be persuasive.

Over time, I've developed a set of future-oriented interjections that draw attention to the future implications of today's decisions. They range from least to most in how heavily they imply the need to make tough near-term decisions. The same variance, of course, applies to the degree of personal risk to the planner in making the intervention:

1. "Well, if we go ahead and do this, *what this means* tomorrow (or next year or three years from now) is _____."

    This is the first level of future-oriented knowledge, understanding the future consequences of today's decision. **What-this-means** observations are extrapolative in nature and, by themselves, not too threatening.

2. "Well, doing this implies or assumes _____, *what if* that turns out not to be the case?"

   What-if questions are more challenging because they both identify underlying assumptions about future demand and question whether those assumptions are valid. It's not too controversial if no one had thought about it in this way; but it's plenty controversial if someone had thought about it but chose not to disclose it.

3. "*But if* tomorrow we find that _____, then doing this won't work."

   But-if assertions put the planner on record as believing that what the organization is deciding to do today will not meet future demand. This not only opposes what somebody (perhaps the CEO) wants to do, but it also calls into question how well somebody understands future demand.

4. "*If* we want to _____ tomorrow, shouldn't we *start* doing _____ today?"

   Planners are on shaky ground when they ask ***if-start*** questions because they are leaving their domain of future demand and entering the supply side of the equation. In effect, they are telling the CEO and his top advisors that they must make a decision to start doing X if they are to meet future demand.

5. "*If* we really want to do _____ tomorrow, we should *stop* doing _____ today."

   Planners should always hope that somebody else steps up to the plate and makes ***if-stop*** assertions, because ultimately the new-start decision will have to identify the bill-payer. When operators fail to make the *stop* decisions, planners need to be cautious in warning that management is only talking the talk, not future making. Operators, particularly the boss, don't like having their seriousness questioned.

Knowing what to say and when to say it is a matter of judgment and intuition. It requires in-depth knowledge of the CEO and his world. A planner who is isolated from the mainstream activities of the organization not only loses the opportunity to represent the future when it really counts but loses the ability to serve effectively as Future Rep. A CEO who hires a planner but doesn't give him or her *access* is wasting money.

Telling the emperor he has no clothes on is never easy, particularly when he or she is the CEO. In his "Confessions of a Trusted Counselor," David A. Nadler, the chairman and CEO of a global management company, was told by Richard Parsons, the CEO of Time Warner, that he knows he doesn't get the whole truth. "For years, Gerry Levin [his predecessor] was one of the guys here I was closest to, but there were just certain issues I was reluctant to bring up to him because he was the CEO. So I have to assume the same thing is happening with people who work for me."[10] As one of the principle obstacles to evidence-based management (that is, making decisions based on facts, not myths, half-truths, poor analogies, etc.) Jeffrey Pfeffer and Robert I. Sutton note what many of us know all too well, that often people simply don't want to hear the truth:

> The phrase *don't shoot the messenger* contains an enormous amount of truth, namely that delivering bad news is not something that typically wins you many friends. People like to deliver good news, regardless of its validity, in large part because most people seem to prefer hearing good news. The important insight here is that a lie takes two parties—the person who tells the lie and quite frequently the listener who signals in a number of ways that she or he wants to be lied to. . . . Building a culture of truth telling and acting on the hard facts requires an enormous amount of self-discipline in order to not only be willing to hear the truth, however unpleasant, but to actually encourage people to deliver the bad news.[11]

Having the fortitude to talk truth to power is a challenge for a subordinate in any hierarchical organization, but if the boss has an "off with their heads" attitude towards the bearers of bad news, he or she will live in wonderland and won't know it's too late until it is too late.

Representing future demand has both a political and an analytic dimension. Articulating the future demand in a manner that results in action is political in nature because it involves persuading an individual who holds an institutional position that changes must be made. The intellectual task is defining *credibly* what the future demand will be. Credibility is always a matter of perception; it depends on the eyes of the beholder. And it's not the perception of the planner that counts; it's the perception of the senior managers. An old friend, once an academic and now an executive vice president at one of the largest defense industry firms, told me that "often planners lose their seat [at the table] because they're dolts who divert decision makers from serious, substantive, truly strategic discussions." This is a tough audience for planners who rest their credibility on their analysis.

Insight and Foresight— Key to Intuiting the Future

The list of analytic tools that generate data about the future— demographic analysis, economic forecasting, technology projections, environmental trends, energy trends, simulations, scenarios, alternative futures, Delphi studies, etc.—is long and getting longer. We planners tend to be analytic types, convinced of our own smarts, and believe that we can use these tools to define future demand. We often persist in this belief despite the poor track record that futurologists have built since the first written word. These analytic tools for understanding the future do provide useful information—for example, we know how many Baby Boomers will retire and when; but they cannot be relied on to provide *the* answer. Only our intuition, as unreliable and partial as it is, can sense when radical changes lurk beneath the surface.

While planners should use analytic tools to provide inputs that shape their mental model of the future, planners should almost never use them in trying to influence how their bosses see the future. Top officials in any organization are intensely and deeply enmeshed in today's reality. There is no end to the fires they have to put out and they have little (if any) time for reflection, much less analysis. Their understanding of today's reality is based on experience and they rely on their intuition in making decisions. They are usually better at deciding what to do than at explaining why. It has been my experience that those who have fought their way to the top of any organization just don't "get" analysis. Planners who rely on analysis in representing the future just typecast themselves (as nerds, according to my VP friend).

T. Irene Sanders is among the most eloquent of those who recognize the role of in-depth knowledge and intuition in understanding change in non-linear systems:

> Successful strategic thinking has two major components: *insight* about the present and *foresight* about the future. And the key to both is understanding the *dynamics* of the "big picture" context in which . . . decisions are being made.[12]

For Sanders, the task of identifying what Andrew Grove calls strategic inflection points demands a systemic perspective, one that focuses on patterns of interactions, relationships and emerging conditions that can lead to paradigm shifts.[13]

In discussing what he was looking for in the management team that would succeed him, General Electric CEO Jack Welch clearly understood the importance and difficulty of future-making bets:

> You've got to bet on what's ahead, not what was done. You've got to sort of get a message from what was done. The whole point is, how are they going to see the future   because seeing tomorrow is what it's all about, not writing a history book.
> Q: So you want someone who has demonstrated a lot of vision, a lot of foresight?
> WELCH: I hope we're able to select a team that has the right combination of foresight and operational skills, because you can't have all foresight and miss out on the numbers. So I hope we can get a team that will have the whole combination.[14]

Foresight about where future demand might go must be grounded in understanding, *but not invested in* how the CEO meets the current demand for an organization's capabilities, products, or services.

From a Meyers-Briggs perspective, planners must rank high on both "sensing" and "intuitive." Planners must gather information, lots of it from lots of sources; but a real understanding of the CEO and his or her world must be grounded in up-close, personal knowledge—"being there" is critical. The knowledge gained from access not only improves the chances that the planner might develop meaningful foresight about future demand, but makes it more likely that the planner can

▲ **Making room at the table for the planner is, in effect, giving the future a seat at the table.**

bring that foresight to the CEO in a persuasive manner. A planner's foresight is wasted if senior management does not share it (even if imperfectly) and act upon it. And often this is a matter of trust as the CEO asks himself, "Am I prepared to take such enormous risks based on what the planner tells me?"

Insight and foresight—both based on human intuition and both certain to fail at some point. But as Heinrich von Pierer (the Siemens CEO who drove the German engineering company's remarkable two-year turnaround in the late 1990s) knows, the New Economy is not for the fainthearted. "In Germany, competition was like a wind. Now it's a storm. And it will become a hurricane. You have to move fast or lose."[15]

Intuition, grounded in experience and aware of the analytic trends, provides the best bet on the future, but no bet is a sure thing. At the same time a firm commits to action, it must be ready to shift course. IBM learned the hard way, when it failed to adapt quickly to fundamental change in the shift to PCs in the market place. Microsoft has internalized it; Bill Gates once asserted that "every new change forces all the companies in an industry to adapt their strategies to that change."[16] Relying on intuition is necessary, but be ready to adapt if it fails.

For the Planner, Some Tough Lessons Learned

The roles of Future Rep and Learning Promoter are closely linked. An effective planner not only has to discern how future demand will evolve but also has to persuade the organization to act on that foresight. It is worth repeating Arie P. De Geus's observation that I cited in Chapter 2: "The only relevant learning in a company is the learning done by those people who have the power to act."

Planners must not only be dispassionate about gauging future demand, but must be dispassionate about their role as well. "Am I adding value?" should be a constant refrain because the CEO doesn't need a planner to make a decision—uninformed decisions get made all the time. At a meeting that I attended, then Air Force chief of staff Ron Fogelman commented, as he reviewed a particularly inept analytic report, that it reminded him of his days as a programmer [the "program" is the Air Force's six-year budget]. He noted that sometimes he would get all the information he could and then make a decision. Other times, he would just make a decision. When he looked back and thought about those decisions he had made with information and those made without it, he concluded that "probably the ones I made with information were better decisions—but not always." The moral—not all informed decisions are the right ones, but the odds of being right improve when your decisions are informed.

Moreover, if a CEO makes a genuinely bad decision (according to one estimate, for example, former Apple Chairman John Sculley's decision not to license the Macintosh operating system in the mid-1980s cost Apple $20 to $40 billion in value[17]), he or she will be taken to task for the decision itself, not for failing to seek the advice of a planner. The planner must always ask, "am I helping my boss do his job, and does he know it?" Some lessons I've learned along the way:

Build Personal Credibility. Speak only when you have something to say. Say something right the first time or risk sounding like a broken record as you labor to be understood. Intervene only on issues that are clearly yours; other members of the CEO's inner circle resent poaching and will try to get you ejected. Don't talk too much because line operators always get weary of listening to staffers before staffers

The Importance of Realism

Larry Bossidy and Ram Charan cite "insist on realism" as one of the "seven essential behaviors" in building a disciplined, execution-focused organization:

> Realism is the heart of execution, but many organizations are full of people who are trying to avoid or shade reality. Why? It makes life uncomfortable. People don't want to open Pandora's Box. They want to hide mistakes, or buy time to figure out a solution rather than admit they don't have an answer at the moment. They want to avoid confrontations. Nobody wants to be the messenger who gets shot or the troublemaker who challenges the authority of her superiors.[1]

For Jim Collins, the leaders of good-to-great companies generally followed the principle that "you absolutely cannot make a series of good decisions without first confronting the brutal facts"—and the comparison companies generally did not.[2] Collins uses Winston Churchill as an inspirational example:

> Armed with this bold vision [of "destroy(ing) Hitler and every last vestige of the Nazi regime"], Churchill never failed, however, to confront the brutal facts. He feared that his towering, charismatic personality might deter bad news from reaching him in its starkest form. So, early in the war, he created an entirely separate department outside the normal chain of command, called the Statistical Office, with the principal function of feeding him—continuously updated and completely unfiltered—the most brutal facts of reality. He relied heavily on this

get tired of talking. The issue is personal credibility—you want the CEO and others at the top to listen when you speak. You know you have succeeded when they ask you what you think.

Maintain an External Focus. The planner's job is to stay focused on future demand, not on how the company will meet that demand. Part of my value to the Air Force stemmed from my previous jobs in the Secretary of Defense's office and the Congress, in effect the "consumers" who provide tax dollars to pay for air power. By stress-

special unit throughout the war, repeatedly asking for facts, just the facts. As the Nazi panzers swept across Europe, Churchill went to bed and slept soundly: "I . . . had no need for cheering dreams," he wrote. "Facts are better than dreams."[3]

For Jeffrey Pfeffer and Robert I. Sutton, a core principle for evidence-based management is the "no brag, just facts" mantra of Da Vita, which operates more than 600 dialysis centers in 37 states:

"No brag, just facts" is the best slogan we know for guiding and inspiring an evidence-based management movement. It is the antidote to the smart talk, self-aggrandizement, and bullshit-based decisions that pollute so much of business life. As Yale's Harry Frankfurt defines it, bullshit means that a person makes assertions with "complete disregard for whether what he's saying corresponds to the facts." If there is to be an evidence-based management movement, at least in your company, it means doing just the opposite. Rather than tolerating half-truths and nonsense, it means that people will hold each other accountable for saying things that correspond to the facts, and as we've emphasized, will act on the best facts even when they are painful to hear.[4]

1 Bossidy and Charan, *Execution: The Discipline of Getting Things Done* (New York, NY: Crown Business, 2002), 67.

2 Collins, *Good to Great: Why Some Companies Make the Leap . . . and Other's Don't* (New York: Harper Business, 2001), 70.

3 Ibid., 73.

4 Pfeffer and Sutton, *Hard Fact, Dangerous Half Truths & Total Nonsense*, 222. ▲

ing consumer needs rather than supplier's advocacy, I brought an external focus to the table.

The CEO is the planner's internal customer, and what the CEO needs from his or her planner is insight into what the company's external customers or consumers will want in the future.

Get Out into the Field. Andrew Grove freely acknowledged that he was one of the last to understand the severity of the Pentium crisis (the impact on Intel's credibility that the discovery of a statistically insignificant error would have) because "most CEOs" are "in the center of a fortified palace and news from the outside has to percolate through layers of people from the periphery where the action is."[18] Planners need to get out in the field and talk to people on the frontline and to the customers they are serving. More CEOs are trying to do this for themselves, but the pressure on their time is too great. Planners need to get out of headquarters, if only to see how the center is viewed from the periphery.

Listen to the Next Generation. It's particularly important to talk to younger employees. Not only do they have fresh ideas, they also have values and perspectives that may be quite different than those at the top. In the Air Force, for example, three- and four-star generals at the top (in their fifties, Vietnam service, the end of the draft, the hollowing-out of the force, the height of the Cold War) and majors (in their early thirties, all-volunteer force, end of the Cold War, the Information Revolution, globalization) have fundamentally different views on issues ranging from why they serve (a calling versus a job) to the future of the Air Force (the younger generation asks why not a separate Space Force). Understanding how future leaders see today's reality provides better insight (and foresight), but it's been my experience that the planner should be very careful on how that knowledge is brought back to the CEO. Nothing irritates an old dog more than the implication that he can't learn new tricks.

▲ **The planner's job is to say, "but, sir" or "what if." You tolerate him or her because it's often too hard for you to ask these questions of yourself.**

Collect Vivid Particulars. Another reason to get out into the field is to collect striking, memorable examples that both make a point and provide material for the boss to use. When listening to a subordinate make her case, senior managers are often visualizing how they themselves would make that case to other senior stakeholders. Providing a startling number to make a point carries a lot more weight than an overall statistical analysis; a vivid example is more memorable than describing a long-term trend. Give the CEO a story, complete with illustrative vivid particulars—which he can use—as it improves the chances that he will adopt your story as his own.

Build Energy Behind an Idea. Organizational learning rarely occurs via an "ah ha!" flash of insight or a road-to-Damascus revelation. In the previously cited example, Andrew Grove and Gordon Moore had an epiphany—get out of memories—but it took them a year to really believe it and take action. The planner has to have a story—you can't beat something with nothing—and has to stay on message. Building energy behind an idea takes time, patience, work, and opportunism. Changing the way an organization prepares for the future usually takes a campaign consisting of many individual encounters with senior stakeholders. The planner's voice by itself is never enough; others have to buy in. The turning point in the campaign usually occurs when the CEO gets on board, but there will still be resistance to overcome. Change is hard, and many battles have to be won before a consensus is built to make it happen.

The planner's job is a staff job. It's expendable by definition. The position carries no authority, but the planner can build personal authority. In fact, he must in order to help the CEO make the organization's future.

For the CEO and His Team, Some (Respectful) Advice

CEOs acting under conditions of great uncertainty face gut-wrenching challenges, namely having the knowledge and courage to commit to decisive action while understanding that his or her bet on the future could be wrong. In *Blown to Bits*, Philip Evans and Thomas S. Wurster argue that the information technology explosion has "deconstructed" the value chain of most industries and created a competitive environment in which the value of winning and the cost of losing have escalated:

The economics of businesses after deconstruction will often be simpler and therefore more powerful: competitive advantage and the distribution of rewards will become much more skewed. Information flows, in particular, will tend to become either value-less or monopolies, and *it really matters* to understand which. If, within a given business, there is room for only one winner, getting strategy *right* becomes really important: *getting it right becomes more important than not getting it wrong.*[19]

A bad decision can be undone; there is no cure for indecisiveness. Former PepsiCo CEO Roger Enrico maintains that "when you are faced with a decision, the best thing is to do the right thing, the next best is to do the wrong thing, and the worst thing is to do nothing."[20] Successful future making requires a CEO who steps up to the plate and makes the tough decisions.

There is no substitute for a strong, decisive CEO. A planner helps by providing a what-if counterpoint to the CEO's main thrust of action. You are paying the planner to take a contrarian view and to nag you about the futurity of your decisions. You give the planner access to ensure that he or she doesn't miss any opportunity for second guessing. Why should you put up with the aggravation? Because your bet on the future could be wrong. That's why you need somebody who knows you and your job, but is not invested in how you are doing your job today. The planner's job is to say, "but, sir" or "what if." You tolerate him or her because it's often too hard for you to ask these questions of yourself.

In a Nutshell

▲ Defining and meeting future demand, not just executing better in meeting today's demand, is critical to the long-term survival of any company.

▲ CEOs usually get to the top by being successful at doing what they are doing today. To be successful tomorrow, they need a dispassionate perspective on future demand, one not concerned about making the future safe for today's way of doing business.

▲ The role of Future Rep is tricky and requires patience and self-restraint on the part of the planner. Making the case too aggressively or in an impolitic manner risks ejection from the inner circle. There is no law that says the planner has to have a seat at the table.

▲ Overcoming denial and promoting truth-telling is critical. The first step in making your organization's future is seeing the present and future as it is, warts and all.

▲ Only human intuition can sense when big changes are coming. A planner's insight about today's reality and foresight about tomorrow's must be grounded in up-close, personal knowledge of the CEO and his or her world.

▲ Planners must be confident of their own abilities but always insecure about whether they are adding value. Their job is to raise inherently uncomfortable "what if" or "but, sir" questions that imply that the CEO is short sighting the future. Being a yes-man is safer, but it doesn't help an organization make its future.

Notes

1 Gary Hamel and Liisa Valikangas, "The Quest for Resilience," *Harvard Business Review* (September 2003), online version reprint, 2.

2 *Business Week* (February 5, 2001), 107–8. Quote is from an excerpt from Jeffrey E. Garten, The Mind of the C.E.O. (New York: Basic Books/Perseus Publishing, 2001).

3 Shawn Young and Joann S. Lublin, "Lucent Ousts McGinn as CEO and Chairman," *Wall Street Journal* (October 24, 2000), B1.

4 Ralph D Stacey, *Managing the Unknowable: Strategic Boundaries between Order and Chaos in Organizations* (San Francisco: Jossey-Bass Publishers, 1990); Margaret J. Wheatley, *Leadership and the New Science: Learning about Organization From an Orderly Universe* (San Francisco: Berret-Koehler Publishers, 1992); Darryl R. Connor, *Leading at the Edge of Chaos: How to Create the Nimble Organization* (New York: John Wiley & Sons, Inc., 1998); T. Irene Sanders, *Strategic Thinking and the New Science: Planning in the Midst of Chaos, Complexity and Change* (New York: The Free Press, 1998).

5 Connor, *Leading at the Edge of Chaos*, vi (see note 4).

6 Phillip Evans and Thomas S. Wurster, *Blown to Bits: How the New Economics of Information Transforms Strategy* (Boston, Mass: Harvard Business School Press, 2000), x.

7 David Streitfeld, "For a Dead Idea, the 'Network Computer' Is Downright Sprightly," *Washington Post* (June 11, 2000), H1.

8 Ariana Eunjung Cha, "New Microsoft Windows Raises Same Old Issues." *Washington Post* (February 14, 2001), E1.

9 Up Front, *Business Week* (March 5, 2001), 14.

10 David A. Nadler, "Confessions of a Trusted Counselor," *Harvard Business Review* (September 2005), online version reprint, 1.

11 Jeffrey Pfeffer and Robert I. Sutton, *Hard Facts, Dangerous Half-Truths, and Total Nonsense: Profiting from Evidence-Based Management* (Boston, MA: Harvard Business School Press, 2006), 32.

12 T. Irene Sanders, *Strategic Thinking and the New Science: Planning in the Midst of Chaos, Complexity and Change* (New York: The Free Press, 1998), 76.

13 Ibid., 78–79.

14 Robert Slater, *The GE Way Fieldbook: Jack Welch's Battle Plan for Corporate Revolution* (New York: McGraw-Hill, 2000), 177.

15 Jack Ewing, "Siemens Climbs Back," *Business Week* (June 5, 2000), 82.

16 John A. Byrne, "Strategic Planning: After a decade of gritty downsizing, big thinkers are back in corporate vogue, *Business Week* (August 26, 1996), online archive version, 3.

17 Ibid.

18 Andrew S. Grove, *Only the Paranoid Survive: How to Exploit the Crisis Points that Challenge Every Company* (New York: Doubleday, 1996), 22.

19 Evans and Wurster, *Blown to Bits,* 224.

20 Jeffrey E. Garten, *The Mind of the C.E.O.* (New York: Basic Books, 2001), 147.

4

Keeping Core Competencies
Relevant to Future Demand

THE CONCEPT OF CORE COMPETENCIES has won widespread usage
since C.K. Prahalad and Gary Hamel's seminal article appeared in
the *Harvard Business Review* in 1990. Companies should no longer
view themselves as a collection of business units but as a portfolio
of core competencies that, if nurtured over time, will give the firm a
sustainable advantage over its competitors. Honda, which developed
its superior ability to build small engines in the Japanese motorcycle
market and then exploited it across many markets (from cars to lawn
mowers) the world over, became the poster child of the core competency movement.[1]

As is often the case with any good idea, there has been some debate over who had it first or what it really means. Peter Drucker, for
example, noted that he had been pushing "strength analysis"—what
does a company do well that gives it a competitive edge—since the
mid-1960s.[2] Noting that Honda has superior competence in several
areas (making engines, managing dealers, and product realization)
not just one (making engines), George Stalk, Philip Evans, and Lawrence E. Shulman argued that it was not a corporation's core competencies but its "capabilities" across the entire value chain that really
mattered.[3] Michael E. Porter took a similar approach in insisting that
"everything matters," not just core competencies or success factors,
because a firm's competitive advantage "comes from the way its activities fit and reinforce one another" across the value chain.[4]

Disney Tries to Sustain its Core Competence

From a core competency perspective, Walt Disney Company's merger with Steve Jobs's Pixar Animation Studios seemed like a no-brainer to several analysts:

> Strategically, we think the deal would make sense since Disney views animation as a key core competency and vital to its future. We believe that Pixar's track record suggests that it has arguably become the pre-eminent name in animation.
> —Katherine Styponias, Prudential[1]

> To me, the deal has the smell of inevitability to it. If it doesn't happen, for whatever reason, it would be a lost opportunity for both companies. The long-term trajectory of both these companies without each other is downwards.
> —Paul Saffo, Institute for the Future[2]

This view, of course, assumes that animation is the competency and that Disney needed to recover from having missed the wave of computer animation. But what if animation wasn't the real competency in question?

The main problem with Disney recently was not technology but that its stories and characters just haven't caught on with the

---

Critics have taken the core competency gurus to task for emphasizing internal factors (identifying what the firm does really well) to the exclusion of external factors (identifying what will sell in future markets). In making their case for competing on the basis of "strategic resources," David J. Collis and Cynthia A. Montgomery first praise and then attack the construct:

> The great contribution of the core competence notion is its recognition that, in corporations with a traditional divisional structure, investment in the corporation's resources often takes a backseat to optimizing current divisional profitability. Core competence, therefore, identifies the critical role that the corporate office has to play as the guardian of what are, in essence, the crown jewels of the corporation.

public as they did in the past. Pixar has had a winner every time and has become what Disney used to be in terms of well-crafted stories, vibrant personalities, warmth and heart.

—John Canemaker, New York University[3]

Addressing a creativity deficit, however, is a lot more difficult than addressing a technology deficit, which, as Steve Jobs observed, really depends on organizational culture: "[Much of the discussion has] been about preserving the Pixar culture because, as you know, that's what's going to determine the success in the long run."[4] Dartmouth College's Anant Sundaram, for one, is skeptical: "One is hard-pressed to find where a much smaller entity comes in and changes a larger entity. What happens is the smaller entity and its modes of operating often get squelched."[5]

---

1 Steven Levingston and Mike Musgrove, "Will Pixar Move In With the Mouse?" *Washington Post* (January 20, 2006), D2.

2 Ibid., D1.

3 Steven Levingston and Mike Musgrove, "Disney to Buy Pixar Studios In Its Move to A Digital Era, *Washington Post* (January 25, 2006), A12.

4 Ibid.

5 Ibid. ▲

At the same time, investing in core competencies without examining the competitive dynamics that determine industry attractiveness is dangerous. By ignoring the marketplace, managers risk investing heavily in resources that will yield low returns.[5]

More recently, Clayton M. Christensen, the creator of the path-breaking concept of disruptive innovation, and Michael E. Raynor observed that the "problem with the core-competence/not-your-core-competence categorization is that what might seem to be a non-core activity today might become an absolutely critical competence to have mastered in a proprietary way in the future." They cite IBM as an example of short-sighted, core competency thinking:

Consider, for example, IBM's decision to outsource the micro-processor for its PC business to Intel, and its operating system to

Microsoft. IBM made those decisions in the early 1980s to focus on what it did best—designing, assembling, and marketing computer systems. Given its history, these choices made perfect sense. Component suppliers to IBM historically had lived a miserable, profit-free existence, and the business press widely praised IBM's decision to outsource these components of its PC. It dramatically reduced the cost and time required for development and launch. And yet in the process of outsourcing what it did not perceive to be core to the new business, IBM put into business the two companies that subsequently captured most of the profit in the industry.[6]

Given the magnitude of this miscalculation, it's not surprising that Christensen and Raynor emphatically conclude: "Core competence, as it is used by many mangers, is a dangerously inward-looking notion. *Competitiveness is far more about doing what customers value than doing what you think you are good at.*"[7]

This makes so much common sense—the last company building nothing but typewriters was undoubtedly very good at it—that one wonders how the core competency gurus could have missed it. The answer, of course, is that they didn't. Prahalad and Hamel, for example, were clear from the get-go that a core competence should "provide potential access to a wide variety of markets" and "make a significant contribution to the perceived customer benefits of the end product."[8]

The debate over whether one should take an internal or external perspective on corporate strategy is overdrawn. All successful practitioners take both; and on a close reading, most analysts, consultants, and professors also do. Everyone agrees that it makes no sense to build superior products, services, or capabilities for which there will be little or no demand. It is not just what an organization *does best* (the internal perspective), but, as discussed above, it's what it does best *that sells* (the external perspective). In fact, the closer one looks at how the core competency construct is actually used, the harder it is to separate the internal and external side of the equation.

Focus, Focus, Focus

The core competency construct had great appeal in the 1990s because American corporations, particularly in the automobile industry, were losing market share. The Japanese simply built cheaper, more reliable, better performing cars. This challenged how American firms produced goods and convinced them they had to get faster, better, and cheaper to meet the competition. The internal emphasis of the core competency approach is not surprising given the American deficit in operational effectiveness at that time. However, most corporate leaders today embrace the "core" idea but attach it, not to the internal competencies of their firm, but to "core" products that dominate their market or "core" businesses in which their products dominate. It's not just focusing on what a firm does well, but focusing on what a firm does well that sells well.

The idea of "focus" and "core business" were the mantras for CEOs trying to pull off corporate turnarounds as the new millennium dawned:

▲ In justification of Xerox's announcement that it was cutting 5,200 jobs, CEO G. Richard Thoman stated: "Xerox can no longer operate business as usual and expect to win. This program is aimed at eliminating activities not associated with our core business functions and strengthening areas that fuel Xerox's growth."[9]

▲ Sara Lee announced that it would sell off several businesses (leather goods, sports attire and food service distribution) to concentrate on three business areas (food and beverages, intimates and underwear, and household products) in, according to the incoming CEO, a "new vision for Sara Lee . . . that will focus our business portfolio and resources."[10]

▲ The giant Anglo-Dutch food conglomerate, Unilever, set out on a new strategy of "focusing on its 400 most successful brands of its roster of more than 1,600 brands."[11]

▲ Flatly labeling his predecessor's effort to diversify Mattel beyond its core toy business a "strategic error," the new Chairman and

CEO, Robert Eckert said: "The theme I'm going to repeat over and over is that Mattel represents the world's premier toy brands today and tomorrow. This tells you what we are. This is what we're going to do for the next 15 years."[12]

Where did this focus on focus begin? Probably with the now legendary former CEO of General Electric, John F. Welch, Jr. When Jack Welch became CEO in 1981, GE had 45 strategic business units, 350 product lines, and employed 404,000 people.[13] In one of his first major speeches on how to grow fast in a slow-growth economy, Welch outlined the "simple *core* [emphasis added] concept that will guide General Electric in the '80s and govern our diverse plans and strategies." He asserted:

> The winners in this slow-growth environment will be those who search out and participate in the real growth industries and insist upon being number one or number two in every business they are in—the number one or number two leanest, lowest-cost, worldwide producers of quality goods and services or those who have a clear technological edge, a clear advantage in a market niche.[14]

During the 1980s, Welch relentlessly applied the number one or number two rule despite the angst (the idea of any home appliance market without a GE product in it was unimaginable to many) and the pain (the workforce was cut back to 229,000) as GE downsized before downsizing was in.[15] When Jack Welch left in 2001, GE was focused on ten business areas and vied regularly with Microsoft and Cisco as the nation's most valuable business.

Welch's number one or number two injunction blends the internal and external perspective—being faster, better, and cheaper only matters if you can be at the top—by focusing the firm's effort on the best markets for its products. This focusing strategy has been widely emulated: Cisco, for example, modeled its strategy after GE. According to CEO John Chambers, "we're like GE in that we want to be No. 1 or No. 2 in all our businesses."[16] In another interview, Chambers elaborated:

Customers Count

Cisco is widely known for its extreme customer focus. Asked what he looks for in his top team, CEO John Chambers identified "customer focus" as a principal requirement: "You've got to say, Does each one of our leaders, regardless of what function they're in, really think 'Customer First'? It's amazing when you go to other companies and you sit in their meetings, how sometimes the word "customer" never comes up. It's actually scary."[1]

Noting that a "leader must walk his or her own talk," Chambers continued: "So if you say customer success is most important, I still listen to every critical account [instances of unstable networks that cause consumer-satisfaction issues) in the world every night."[2] Fortune reported that Chambers spends 30 hours a week or more in meetings with customers and makes sure that his team shares his customer focus:[3] "Then we pay every manager on customer satisfaction. It's amazing how that works. Once you say it's going to be part of their compensation, people say, 'This must really be important,' and, secondly, 'John's going to ask me about it all the time.' And for either reason, they respond very well."[4]

Chambers believes that in the Internet economy "everything gets cheaper forever" because consumers can instantly compare prices from producers the world over, thus making customer focus mandatory for everyone: "keeping your finger on the pulse of your customer will become a requirement. Customer priorities will change so rapidly and what [customers] will pay a premium for will commoditize so rapidly that if you don't have your finger on their pulse, you're going to be in trouble."[5]

---

1 Scott Thurm, "How to Drive an Express Train," *Wall Street Journal* (June 2, 2000), B4.

2 Ibid.

3 Andy Serwer, "There's Something About Cisco," *Fortune* (May 15, 2000), 134.

4 Thurm, "How to Drive," *Wall Street Journal*, B4.

5 John A. Byrne, "Visionary vs. Visionary," *Business Week* (August 28, 2000), 210. ▲

The approach that we started in '93 was one of segmenting the market, being No.1 and No.2 in each segment and each product area . . . and [devising] our strategy to make that happen. . . . [We were] very much focused on how we used systems to gain competitive advantage.[17]

The message for all CEOs seems quite simple: focus on high pay-off areas in which you can do well.

In his definitive study of good-to-great companies, Jim Collins, at first blush, seems to be an internal focus proponent when he argues that a great company is a hedgehog who knows one big thing, unlike foxes who know many things, and know that "if you cannot be the best in the world at your core business, then your core business cannot form the basis of your Hedgehog Concept."[18] But the process by which great companies become great is very externally focused:

The good-to-great leaders understood three simple truths. First, if you begin with "who" rather than "what," you can more easily adapt to a changing world. . . . Second, if you have the right people . . . the problem of how to motivate and manage people largely goes away. . . . Third, if you have the wrong people, it doesn't matter whether you discover the right direction, you *still* won't have a great company. Great vision without great people is irrelevant.

All good-to-great companies began the process of finding a path to greatness by confronting the brutal factors of their current reality. When you start with an honest and diligent effort to determine the truth of your situation, the right decisions often become self-evident. It is impossible to make good decisions without infusing the entire process with an honest confrontation of the brutal facts.[19]

Collins's analysis underscores that good-to-great leaders build the best-in-the-world capabilities (primarily people and processes) before deciding on "what" their company will be best at, and that "what" is based on "piercing insight into how to most effectively generate sustained and robust cash flow and profitability."[20] Not surprisingly, given this blending of the internal and external focus, Collins

The Downside of Strategic Focus
as described by Jeffrey Pfeffer and Robert I. Sutton:

Focus is great. But it can create blinders. In a world of uncertainty and change, and in an organizational world in which everyone, including senior management, is inevitably fallible, too much focus and too little peripheral vision leaves organizations susceptible to being replaced in the marketplace by new entrants or more nimble competitors. Take a look at *Winning Through Innovation* by Michael Tushman and Charles O'Reilly, which lists industry after industry— everything from watches, to cement, to tires, to airlines—where strong incumbents were displaced by newcomers and upstarts. The rise and fall of leading companies is a well-known story. But the role of too much strategic focus in this inability to maintain competitive advantage is a part of the tale that is all too infrequently told.[1]

That's Why the CEO Needs a Planner
by Clark Murdock:

This propensity to stay focused on what one does well, rather than what sells, reflects the all-too-human tendency to make the future safe for how we do business today. Microsoft and Apple make PCs—so Bill Gates, who once commented that the PC was the best tool mankind ever created, and Steve Jobs, for whom the PC was the "sun,"[2] naturally saw PCs at the center of the future of computing. Oracle and Sun, on the other hand, make large servers for the Internet; so Larry Ellison and Scott McNeal, not surprisingly, believed the Internet would be the future computer. In many cases, firms fail because they are too invested in today's way of meeting current demand. That's why I believe a CEO needs a dispassionate planner who represents future demand. It's also why Pfeffer and Sutton believe that a CEO needs a "blunt friend, mentor, or counselor" to help "see yourself and your organizations as outsiders do."[3]

---

1 Pfeffer and Sutton, *Hard Facts, Dangerous Half-Truths & Total Nonsense: Profiting from Evidence-Based Management* (Boston, MA: Harvard Business School Press, 2006), 149.

2 Peter Burrows, "Apple," *Business Week* (July 31, 2000), 113.

3 Pfeffer and Sutton, 224. ▲

notes in a footnote that "over half the good-to-great companies had some version of the 'number one, number two' concept in place years before it became a management fad."[21]

For CEOs, focus is critical in both deciding *what* to do and *how* to do it. Former IBM CEO Lou Gerstner believes that "there is no question that a good portion of our success was due to all of the deals we *didn't* do," because turnarounds fueled by acquisition usually fail because "a company [that] strays from its core competencies" suffers "a lack of focus" and "ultimately sinks into a deeper hole."

> The fact is, in most cases a company has a set of competitive advantages in its base business. It may be hard—very hard—to redirect or reenergize an existing enterprise. Believe me, it's a lot easier than throwing that enterprise over the fence into a totally new environment and succeeding. Age-old common sense: Stick to your knitting; dance with the partner who brought you. History shows that truly great and successful companies go through constant and sometimes difficult self-renewal of the base business. They don't jump into new pools where they have no sense of the depth or temperature of the water.[22]

The gurus of execution, former Honeywell CEO Larry Bossidy and business consultant Ram Charan, believe that a "leader who says 'I've got 10 priorities' doesn't know what he's talking about":

> Leaders who execute focus on a very few clear priorities that everyone can grasp. Why just a few? First, anybody who thinks through the logic of a business will see that focusing on three or four priorities will produce the best results from the resources at hand. Second, people in contemporary organizations need a small number of clear priorities to execute well. . . . When decision making is decentralized or highly fragmented, as in a matrix organization, people at many levels have to make endless trade-offs. There's competition for resources, and ambiguity over decision rights and working relationships. Without carefully thought-out and clear priorities, people can get bogged down in warfare over who gets what and why.[23]

This widespread acceptance of the need to focus is illustrated in the October 2006 so-called "Peanut Butter Manifesto" from Yahoo senior executive Brad Gralinghouse who, according to *The Wall Street Journal,* argued that the company was "spreading its resources like peanut butter on bread, thinly and evenly across all its activities" and thus "focus[ed] on nothing in particular." Gralinghouse believed that Yahoo lacked a "focused, cohesive vision," which meant it wanted "to do everything and be everything—to everyone."[24] Focus, to be sure, is critical, but is a vision, even a focused one, the way to get it?

Having a Vision Matters

How important is it to have a "vision"? Gary Hamel and C.K. Prahalad believe that companies must have foresight, "a well-articulated point of view about tomorrow's opportunities and challenges," but are clearly skeptical about corporate visioning:

> Visions that are as grandiose as they are poorly conceived deserve to be criticized, as do companies that seem to prefer rhetoric to action. All too often, "the vision" is no more than window dressing for a CEO's ego-driven acquisition binge. Chrysler's purchase of an Italian maker of exotic sports cars and its acquisition of a jet aircraft manufacturer were driven more by the ego and whim of the company's erstwhile chairman, Lee Iacocca, than by a solid, well-founded point of view about what it would take to succeed in the automotive business ten years hence. . . . Any vision that is simply an extension of the CEO's ego is dangerous. On the other hand, it is equally simplistic and dangerous to reject the very notion of foresight simply because some corporate leaders can't distinguish between vanity and vision.[25]

Foresight about future demand is important, but I believe it is not the vision itself. The vision comes from the supply side of the equation and defines what the firm will be and do at some future point. How well that vision positions the firm for the future depends, among other things, on how well it gauges future demand, but the

Knowing Where You Are Going Always Matters

Former IBM CEO Louis V. Gerstner, Jr. on "Strategic Clarity":

> Remember the old saying: "If you don't know where you are going, any road will get you there."
>
> No sports team can score if the players don't know what play is called. If everyone has to think about what to do before acting, then confusion and ineptitude are inevitable.
>
> Companies that out-execute their competitors have communicated crystal-clear messages to all their employees: "This is our mission." "This is our strategy." "This is how you carry out your job."[1]

Jim Collins on good-to-great companies:

> The essential strategic difference between the good-to-great and comparison companies lay in two fundamental distinctions. First, the good-to-great companies founded their strategies on deep understanding along three key dimensions. . . .
>
> 1. *What you can be best in the world at* (and, equally important, what you *cannot* be the best in the world at). . . .
>
> 2. *What drives your economic engine.* . . .
>
> 3. *What you are deeply passionate about.* . . .

CEO's vision must address how the firm intends to meet the future demand for its products, services, or capabilities.

In today's era of rapid, discontinuous change organizations must be able to change and adapt to new circumstances. If they can't change *themselves,* they won't last. A CEO's vision for how the organization needs to change is critical because it provides direction and alignment to those at the top of an organization. The real target for any "vision document" must be the senior stakeholders, not the entire membership of the organization. Once a CEO gets buy-in for his vision from those who make the decisions, and they start acting according to the vision, the actions of those at the top will bring the rest of the organization along. Those at the periphery or the bottom

> Second, the good to great companies translated that under-standing into a simple, crystalline concept that guided all their efforts—hence the term Hedgehog Concept.[2]

Michael E. Porter on the focus and discipline of "strategic positioning":

> Having a strategy is a matter of discipline. It requires a strong focus on profitability rather than just growth, an ability to define a unique value proposition, and a willingness to make tough trade-offs in choosing what not to do. A company must stay the course, even during times of upheaval, while constantly improving and extending its distinctive positioning. Strategy goes far beyond the pursuit of best practices. It involves the configuration of a tailored value chain—the series of activities required to produce and deliver a product or service—that enables a company to offer unique value. To be defensible, moreover, the value chain must be highly integrated [so that it cannot be easily imitated by competitors].[3]

---

1 Louis V. Gerstner, Jr., *Who Says Elephants Can't Dance? Inside IBM's Historic Turn-around* (New York: Harper Business, 2002), 233.

2 Jim Collins, *Good to Great: Why Some Companies Make the Leap...and Others Don't* (New York: Harper Business, 2001), 95–96.

3 Michael E. Porter, "Strategy and the Internet," *Harvard Business Review* (March 2001) online reprint version. ▲

of any organization usually react to what those at the top do, not what they say.

The central purpose of an organization's vision is to get the CEO and his team marching to the same drum. And, as Intel Chairman Andrew Grove illustrates, the key is *focus:*

Management writers use the word "vision" for this. That's too lofty for my taste. What you're trying to do is capture the essence of the company and the focus of its business. You are trying to define what the company will be, yet that can only be done if you also undertake to define what the company will *not be.*[26]

Andrew Grove speaks with the authority of one who has been there and learned the hard way. Comparing organizations facing a strategic crisis to being in "the valley of death," he asks:

> How can you hope to mobilize a large team of employees to pull together, accept new and different job assignments, work in an uncertain environment and work hard despite the uncertainty of their future, if the leader can't or won't articulate the shape of the other side of the valley? . . . Clarity of direction, which includes describing what we are going after as well as describing what we will *not* be going after, is exceedingly important at the late stage of a strategic transformation.[27]

People need to know where they are going during times of great uncertainty, change, and risk. Knowing the end-state is like knowing the destination of a journey—you might not know what challenges you will face or how long it will take you, but you will know when you have reached the end. Odysseus knew where he wanted to go after the Trojan War—home to Ithaca—but had no idea of the hardships he would endure or the ten years it would take him. He just knew where he wanted to go.

Andrew Grove is not alone in being uncomfortable with the "vision thing." That's because most visions are positive, aspiration heavy, feel-good statements full of new-start possibilities. They are *unfocused* because they don't specify where the organization is not going and thus provide no "stop" possibilities. A vision must be *clear* and *specific* if it is to provide meaningful guidance to action.

▲ **Visions, plans, decisions—all statements of intent. Unless followed by action, they are destined to be empty words.**

It must help people decide what to do every day. There is a crude simplicity to many injunctions: be number 1 or number 2 in everything you do; get out of memories and become a microcomputer company; contain the communists; and return to Ithaca—but they help people decide what to do and what not to do. That's the bottom line for any vision—can the vision words be translated into actions?

But It's Actions that Really Count

Visions, plans, decisions—all statements of intent. But unless followed by action, they are destined to become empty words. Actions always speak louder than words.

Walking the future-making walk is always hard. Taking future-oriented actions is even tougher in today's what-have-you-done-for-me-lately economy in which a quarterly earnings statement that failed to meet expectations can drive down stock values. In a penetrating commentary, *Business Week's* Louis Lavelle noted Harvard Business School professor Gary Hamel's discovery that almost half of the companies that raised earnings at least five times faster than sales from 1993 to 1996 (totaling 10 percent of Standard & Poor's top 500) subsequently suffered big drops in earnings growth.[28] Lavelle puts part of the blame on investors "rewarding quarterly earnings gains with a runup in stock price" for the lack of future-oriented decision making:

> Basically, it's the triumph of short-term thinking over planning for the long haul. The cost-cutting measures that may generate a quick earnings boost can make it difficult or impossible for companies to engage in the kind of radical innovation necessary for survival.[29]

Matching deeds to words is the bottom line for future making. For Andrew Grove, the focus on action is so great that his discomfort with the "vision thing" extends to "the planning thing:"

> Strategic *plans* are statements of what we intend to do. Strategic *actions* are steps we have already taken or are taking which suggest our longer-term intent. Strategic *plans* sound like a political speech. Strategic *actions* are concrete steps. . . . While strategic *plans* are abstract and are usually couched in language that has no concrete meaning except to the company's management, strategic *actions* matter because they immediately affect people's lives. . . . Strategic *plans* deal with events that are so far in the future that they have little relevance to what you actually have to do today. So they don't command true attention. . . . Strategic *actions*, however

take place in the present. Consequently, they command immediate attention.[30]

Most of us need visions to have some sense of where we are going. And most of us need plans to have some sense of how we are going to get there. But the real product of future-making planning is decisions about what to start doing to meet future demand and what to stop doing to make room for the future. Making the right strategic decisions, of course, is critical and will be addressed in Chapter 7; but for decisions to matter, they must be followed by action. It's not what we say that counts; it's what we do.

In a Nutshell

▲ The future-making debate over one's core competencies should start by asking what the future demand for our products, services, or capabilities will be. Future makers must then ask themselves if today's core competencies are relevant to future demand.

▲ The debate over whether one should take an internal or external perspective on corporate strategy is overdrawn—most practitioners, analysts, consultants, and professors take both. It's not just what an organization does best (the internal perspective), but it's what it does best that sells (the external perspective).

▲ GE CEO Jack Welch's injunction to stay only in markets in which you can be number one or number two underscores the importance of focus. The message is simple—focus on high payoff areas in which you can do well; avoid low payoff areas no matter how well you do them—but execution is hard (and will be addressed in Chapter 6).

▲ Visions are critical for organizations during times of great uncertainty, change, and risk. People need to know where they are going and when they have reached the end of their journey. The real target for any vision document must be the senior stakeholders because it is critical to get the CEO and his team marching to the same drum.

▲ Taking future oriented actions is tough in today's what-have-you-done-for-me-lately economy. The future making bottom line for any vision is whether the vision can be translated into actions that better prepare the organization for future demand.

Notes

1 C. K. Prahalad and Gary Hamel, "The Core Competence of the Corporation," *Harvard Business Review* (May–June 1990), 79–91.

2 Peter F. Drucker, *Managing in a Time of Great Change* (New York: Truman Talley Books, 1995), 43.

3 George Stalk, Philip Evans and Lawrence E. Shulman, "Competing on Capabilities: The New Rules of Corporate Strategy," *Harvard Business Review* (March–April 1992), 66.

4 Michael E. Porter, "What is Strategy?" *Harvard Business Review* (November–December 1996), 70.

5 David J. Collis and Cynthia A. Montgomery, "Competing on Resources: Strategy in the 1990s," *Harvard Business Review* (July 1995), online reprint version).

6 Clayton M. Christensen and Michael E. Raynor, *The Innovator's Solution: Creating and Sustaining Successful Growth* (Boston, MA: Harvard Business School Press, 2003), 125–126.

7 Ibid., 162.

8 Prahalad and Hamel, "The Core Competence of the Corportation," 83–84.

9 Claudia H. Deutsch, "Xerox to Take $625 Million Write-Off and Eliminate 5,200 Jobs, *New York Times* (April 1, 2000), C1.

10 David Barboza, "Sara Lee Plans to Reorganize Some Apparel and Food Units," *New York Times* (May 31, 2000), C1.

11 Ernest Beck, "Still Hungry, Unilever Faces Full Plate Now," *Wall Street Journal* (May 31, 2000), C1.

12 Lisa Bannon, "Mattel's New Boss Promises a Learner and Meaner Firm," *Wall Street Journal* (August 10, 2000), B2.

13 Robert Slater, *The GE Way Fieldbook: Jack Welch's Battle Plan for Corporate Revolution* (New York: McGraw-Hill, 2000), 7.

14 Ibid., 194–195.

15 Ibid., 7.

16 Andy Serwer, "There's Something About Cisco," *Fortune* (May 15, 2000), 120.

17 Scott Thurm, "How to Drive an Express Train," *Wall Street Journal* (June 2, 2000), B1.

18 Jim Collins, *Good to Great: Why Some Companies Make the Leap...and Others Don't* (New York, NY: Harper Business, 2001), 118.

19 Ibid., 42, 88.

20 Ibid., 95–96.

21 Ibid., 69.

22 Louis V. Gerstner, *Who Said Elephants Can't Dance: Inside IBM's Historic Turnaround* (New York, NY: Harper Business, 2002), 220–221.

23 Larry Bossidy and Ram Charan, *Execution: The Discipline of Getting Things Done* (New York, NY: Crown Business, 2002), 69.

24 Kevin J. Delaney, "As Yahoo Falters, Executive's Memo Calls for Overhaul," *Wall Street Journal* (November 18–19, 2006), A1, A7.

25 Gary Hamel and C.K. Prahalad, *Competing for the Future* (Boston, MA: Harvard Business School Press, 1994), 74–75.

26 Andrew S. Grove, *Only the Paranoid Survive: How to Exploit the Crisis Points that Challenge Every Company* (New York, NY: Currency/Doubleday, 1999), 140.

27 Ibid., 153.

28 Louis Lavelle, "Corporate Liposuction Can Have Nasty Side Effects," *Business Week* (July 17, 2000), 74.

29 Ibid., 74–75.

30 Grove, *Only the Paranoid Survive,* 146–147.

5

How to Keep Innovating

THE IMPERATIVE TO INNOVATE appears to be getting stronger since the turn of the century (when I wrote the first draft of this book). At first, it was about surviving during an era of rapid, discontinuous change, because, by definition, what works today won't work tomorrow. For Andy Grove, it's technological change that is the driver. He has described the line "technology will always win" as Grove's Law, and said: "If the new technology is compelling enough, it will win out. When the railroads came, Wells Fargo was in trouble. When the printing press can along, the monks didn't stay around very long."[1] Then-outgoing CEO for Sun Microsystems, Scott G. McNealy, put it more pithily: "In our business, you innovate or you die."[2]

Now it's the nature of innovation that forces organizations to innovate. Clayton M. Christensen, the 21st century guru of innovation, and his co-authors have examined the question in multiple books. They are at pains to avoid limiting the notion of innovation to technological developments, instead, defining innovation as virtually anything that improves or adds to a company's "resources, processes or values."[3] For our purposes here, the fundamental and useful distinction they make is between sustaining and disruptive innovation. Here is how the distinction is presented in *Seeing What's Next*:

> Sustaining innovations essentially take a good product and make it better and are crucial to a company's growth and prosperity.
>
> However, firms almost always improve their products faster than customer needs can change to use the new innovations.

Therefore, incumbent firms tend to create new products and services at a pace . . . that outstrips the ability of customers . . . to use the improvements.

Disruptive products or services initially are inferior to existing offerings in the attribute that matters most in the mainstream. However, they are typically more affordable and simpler to use than products in the incumbent's product portfolio.

Disruptive innovations typically pose difficulties for an industry's incumbent leaders, who are faced with the choice of investing to improve their products along the sustaining trajectory or investing in disruptive innovations. The choice is difficult because sustaining innovations appear to be much more attractive than disruptive ones, even though disruptive innovations often ultimately drive more long-term growth.[4]

We see that the Christensen world of innovation is also the one the Future Rep inhabits. It continually presents the question, What do we stop doing now and start doing from now on? The Future Rep, who is not responsible for current operations, is well positioned to provide a picture of the future that shows what kind of innovation is needed.

Innovation has also become a business strategy, as large firms in the information age have made it an integral part of their growth strategy. General Electric CEO Jeffrey R. Immelt, who insists that innovation is the "central necessity" of modern business,[5] committed GE in its 2004 annual report "to an average organic growth rate of 8% — that is, growth exclusive of acquisitions at a rate two to three times faster than the growth of world output" despite the fact that, as *Harvard Business Review* editor Thomas A Stewart observes, "no big company has ever sustained organic growth at that pace."[6] Immelt, however, thought he had no choice:

After I came in as CEO, I looked at the world post 9/11 and realized that over the next ten or 20 years, there just was not going to be much tailwind. It would be a more global market, it would be more driven by innovation, and a premium would be placed on companies that could generate their own growth. We have to change the company—to become more innovation driven—in order to deal with this new environment.[7]

In response to Stewart's observation that the "first big thing" he did as CEO was to put a billion dollars into R&D as an "attention-getting growth bet," Immelt said he had to "put a stake in the ground about products, innovation, and technology, because there we could lean into an existing infrastructure that was decent but needed to get out of the basement."[8] Noting that IBM had made its 8% goal for organic revenue growth rate in 2005 and would make in 2006, Immelt concluded his *HBR* interview on an almost messianic note:

> Achieving this kind of growth depends on making it the personal mission of everyone here. . . . . If I want people to take more risks, solve bigger problems, and grow the business in a way that's never been done before, I have to make it personal. . . . This is not a place for small-timers. Working at GE is the art of thinking and playing big; our managers have to work cross function, cross region, cross company. And we have to be about big purposes. We *can* solve health care. . . . If you win here . . . you get to be in the front seat of history, creating the future.[9]*

As will be discussed shortly, "being big" helps when it comes to innovation, but it now appears "being big" means you *have* to innovate to keep growing.

Despite the increasing emphasis on innovation as *the* 21st century corporate strategy, understanding that innovation is important is hardly new. In the September–October 1992 *Harvard Business Review*, Peter F. Drucker, the intellectual godfather of many business strategists (including myself), stated in no uncertain terms that:

---

* Whew! Good thing Jeffrey Immelt was out changing the world—"future creating" is awfully close to *future making*. Shortly after drafting this section, I heard a radio ad (on WTOP, FM 103.5) on April 20, 2007 that ended with the announcer's punch line: "Northrop Grumman—Creating the Future." On the same day, Nancy LeaMond, strategic planner for AARP, responded to a question at a conference hosted by the Global Strategic Initiative (at my think tank, the Center for Strategic and International Studies) that AARP had learned that "the best way to predict the future was to make it." I hope she hasn't expressed this in print somewhere, but it does underscore the point—future making is everywhere.

[The modern organization] must be organized for innovation and innovation, as the great Austro-American economist Joseph Schumpeter said, is "creative destruction." And it must be organized for the systematic abandonment of whatever is established, customary, familiar, and comfortable, whether that is a product, service, or process; a set of skills; human and social relationships; or the organization itself. In short, it must be organized for constant change. The organization's function is to put knowledge to work—on tools, products, and processes; on the design of work; on knowledge itself. It is the nature of knowledge that it changes fast and that today's certainties always become tomorrow's absurdities.[10]

What giants like Peter Drucker may have always known is now becoming common knowledge. A *Business Week* editorial on the "working principles" for the 21st Century Corporation underscores that it's all innovation, all the time:

In an information economy, companies can gain an edge through new ideas and products that increase in value as more people use them. There's no limit to how many people can use idea-based assets, such as the Palm Pilot or America Online's instant-messaging system. Information-based products can reward early leaders with temporary monopolies and winner-take-all profits. But the emphasis is on "temporary." Knowledge-based products and networks can quickly disappear in a burst of Schumpeterian creative destruction. So corporations must innovate rapidly and continuously.[11]

The key to making *Fortune*'s list of the world's Most Admired Companies in 2000 was the ability to constantly innovate.[12] Cisco CEO John Chambers certainly understood the information age imperative to innovate: "At Cisco, we have encouraged a culture that embraces speed and change. What our customers think of as our primary added-value has changed seven times in the past decade. Our challenge is to stay abreast and even drive the transformation of the global economy."[13] Clayton Christensen and Michael Raynor believe that "instead of asking what their company does best today, managers should ask, "What do we need to master today, and what will we need to master in the future, in order to excel on the trajectory of improvement that customers will define as important?"[14]* How to keep innovating, the subject of this chapter, appears to be an enduring challenge.

Giving the Future a Seat at the Table—
The Planner's Role

Management professor and consultant Gary Hamel believes that the bottleneck to learning about the future and to change is the "tyranny of experience" at the top of the organizational pyramid (see Chapter 1), and we should stop "celebrating the exceptions—the few truly transformational executives who populate every tome on leadership."[15] It is undeniable that we humans have more difficulty learning and adapting as we grow older (although you *can* teach an old dog new tricks). It is also hard for us not to be emotionally invested in and psychologically attached to the things that have brought us great success. The much-quoted former Intel CEO Andy Grove, for example, believes that the high turnover in CEOs reflects the inability of the top team to avoid this trap:

> I suspect that the people coming in are probably no better managers or leaders than the people they are replacing. They have only one advantage, but it may be crucial: unlike the person who has devoted his entire life to the company and therefore has a history of deep involvement in the sequence of events that led to the present mess, the new managers come unencumbered by such emotional involvement and therefore are capable of applying an impersonal logic to the situation. They can see things much more objectively than their predecessors did.[16]

Humans do not stop being humans when they become senior managers. Asking any of us, including those at the top of any organi-

---

* There it is again—"future mastering" is *really* close to future making.

zation, to be truly dispassionate and objective about who we are and what we are doing is often asking too much. As management expert Jay R. Galbraith of Galbraith Associates observed of a post-Grove Intel that generates almost $1 billion a month in profits: "Change is really hard when you're solidly on top. . . .He'll [Intel CEO Paul S. Otellini] have to bring in new people who have new skill sets."[17]

It is not just the "tyranny of experience" that makes it hard for senior managers to learn about the future; it's also the tyranny of the in-box. Time is the scarcest resource for any senior executive. Real learning about the future—that is, learning that leads to action—takes time. It can't be done on the fly or squeezed into an already overbooked schedule. A CEO must carve out time, both personal and organizational, for learning about and preparing for the future. A planning process, as well as the planner who manages it, can help an organization make time for effective future making.

How does the planner help her boss learn about the future? Let's assume she has been empowered, both with direct access to the CEO and with a planning process. She has spent time in the field and talked to everybody, particularly the younger and newer members of the organization. She knows where the senior stakeholders stand and really believes that her foresight about the future demand for the organization's services is on the mark. The planning off-site is scheduled. How does she promote sufficient learning about the future to get her bosses to take ownership of the need to change? My experience suggests the following guidelines for the planner:

Planning events must work as events. Your off-site participants are all too aware of the opportunity costs they are incurring—crises left unattended, phone calls unanswered, e-mails piling up, etc. They need to be entertained and they need to feel they have accomplished something. They also need to be active participants with speaking roles. Planners too often make all of the presentations in the mistaken belief that it's more important to get the substance exactly right than to have a lively exchange that's somewhat off the point (in the planner's view). Leave plenty of time for off-line discussion because everybody comes with a non-planning agenda they need to work.

Always focus on making the planning event succeed as an event, even at the expense of planning content.

Make sure the No. 1 participant is primed and engaged. The personal enthusiasm and involvement of the senior participant is critical to the success of the event. Principals hate being surprised, and if caught off guard, are likely to take it out on the planner who, after all, is responsible for the event. *You must get on your boss's calendar before the off-site and make sure that he or she is on board.* At the event itself, the attendees take their cues from the top dog. One of the four-star chairs of the Air Force's planning board of directors (the BoD membership included key three-star generals and senior civilian officials) was fond of comparing the day-long BoD meetings to a "dentist appointment: I always look forward to them with dread, but once endured, I'm always glad that I went." Not the most positive of images. The life slowly leaked out of the BoD until a new chair (who had been a participant during the planning-as-dentistry phase) disbanded it. In this instance, we planners violated the first rule—the BoD didn't work as an event for the new chair. The attitude and energy of your boss is critical; no planning event will succeed without his or her active, supportive participation. A future-oriented CEO is not produced by the off-site itself, but by your "care and feeding" of the CEO before the off-site.

Making the future real. Future making is not just talking about the future; it's about taking actions today that better prepare the organization to meet future demand. As a planner, you have to get your leadership's head into the future and make its opportunities and threats seem real. Use anything—a provocative futurist, visualization techniques, seminar games, simulations, trend analysis, etc.—that gets the participants talking about and living in the future. Get the CEO to endorse a no-Blackberry zone to ensure that participants stay focused on the future, not today's in-box. It's a good idea to pretest everything to see what works but be sure to pre-test with senior-level officials. It was my experience that techniques that worked well with colonels (for example, a seminar war game) often flopped with three-stars (they were too busy playing themselves to play game roles).

Making the future real, giving it taste and texture, is challenging work, but critical—no one takes actions today to prepare for tomorrow unless one feels the presence of the future.

Get decisions made at the planning event. Top executives don't plan to plan or believe that it's simply the act of planning that matters. They want to accomplish something. So your event must have an action agenda that requires decisions from them. Ask for guidance or direction even if you might not like the direction you are sent in. Your leadership needs to believe that it's their planning process, not yours. Ask for decisions that empower change, that provide someone with ammunition to get resources ("At the off-site, the boss told me to start doing X"). Your chances of getting a future-oriented decision are higher at an event that is focused on the future. Be aggressive—turn observations about the future into questions seeking decisions. Close the meeting with a recap of the decisions made, using it (if you have left enough time) as an opportunity to get more decisions on open issues. You need to be pro-active in facilitating strategic decision-making because the payoff for the planner is so high—making decisions gives the participants a sense of accomplishment, and the decisions themselves are your levers for change. You will overstep your limits from time to time, but you may be surprised at how many decisions you can get if you just ask for them.

▲ **An organization hasn't really learned anything about the future unless it acts on that knowledge—this is the bottom line of future making.**

An organization hasn't really learned anything about the future unless it acts on that knowledge—this is the bottom line of future making. While it is actions that count, decisions usually precede them. Planning events are opportunities for getting an organization's head into the future. They are also the best time to get future-oriented decisions because that's when the grip of the future is the strongest. Future making doesn't stop here—decisions, like plans, have to be implemented—but making an organization's future requires future-oriented decisions.

Investing in the Future—The CEO's Job

How much should organizations invest in the future? Peter F. Drucker believes that organizations seeking to survive during periods of rapid, structural change should devote 10 to 12 percent of their resources (during good and bad times) to a "budget for the future" that funds a "systematic policy of innovation, that is, a policy to create change."[18] Corning, for example, puts 10 percent of sales into R&D.[19] Sun Microsystems bounced back from the 2000–2001 telecom implosion because Sun, according to then-CEO Scott McNealy, "took the peak-of-the-bubble R&D level and maintained it, even though revenue came down. This year [2005], we're going to spend $2.2 billion."[20] No one really knows how much is enough for innovation, but it's clearly a lot more than nothing.

Innovation via acquisition—also known as "checkbook R&D"—is easier if you are big. Former GE CEO Jack Welch stated at his 1999 annual meeting:

> But there is one huge **advantage** in being a big company and that is in **using** size rather than trying to manage it—taking swings, lots of them, with the confidence that comes from knowing that, unlike many smaller companies, an occasional miss, even a big miss, does not mean the end of the game. We made 108 acquisitions in 1998, for $21 billion, and have averaged over 70 per year for the past five years. The vast majority have been successful, but naturally, a few have not turned out as planned. But it is the pace and intensity of the acquisitions that our size permits, and the knowledge that a "miss" won't be fatal, that keeps GE growing and moving forward.[21]

If you are big, you buy the ideas and talent necessary for innovation. Microsoft CEO Steve Ballmer said in mid-2006 that it had acquired 22 companies over the past year, and IBM made 16 acquisitions in 2005. According to Advanced Technology Ventures' Wes Raffel, both "have big war chests for acquisitions" and are prowling Silicon Valley looking for start-ups.[22] As Jack Welch told analysts in April 2000: "It isn't about revolution. It's about [being] bigger, taking risk. You almost can't screw this thing up, it's so big and powerful."[23]

▲ Incentivizing Innovation

Business Week observed in mid-2005 that companies as varied as Motorola, Mattel, Steelcase, and Boeing were establishing innovation labs, where employees from across the company are brought together in off-site locations to form "mosh pits" of creativity.[1] Even the Silicon-based Yahoo! Inc., set up its own in-house incubator in San Francisco, known as Brickhouse, which is led by Caterina Fake, co-founder of a start-up that Yahoo acquired in mid-2005, who said: "Brickhouse gives us the ability to capture all the cool, inventive ideas they've [the so-called "rock stars" of amazing talent and creativity] got and develop them."[2]

IBM, which started using online, company-wide brainstorming sessions in 2001, conducted an "Innovation Jam" in 2006, which brought together over 100,000 people, both from within and outside IBM (including clients, customers and even competitors) to first look for new ideas and then to refine them in two 72-hour sessions on four topics: transportation, health, the environment, and finance and commerce.[3] For IBM, whose mid-2007 motto is "Innovation That Matters" and whose self-definition includes "The Innovators' Innovator," this grass-roots approach to innovation is a no-brainer.

Procter & Gamble is even more aggressive about seeking good ideas wherever they are and has moved from R&D to what they call its C&D or "connect and develop" innovation model:

> With a clear sense of consumers' needs, we could identify promising ideas throughout the world and apply our own R&D,

Most organizations, however, do not have the resources to simply buy the ideas that prevailed in the fierce competition between start-ups. And even those firms with large R&D checkbooks must develop innovation-friendly climates to ensure that the ideas and talent they bought flourish and not wither in their new environs. The planner has helped the CEO to understand what the future demand will be; it is the CEO's job to make sure that the organization takes advantage of that foresight. Building a company that innovates—the only ones that survive in the New Economy—requires the following:

manufacturing, marketing, and purchasing capabilities to them to create better and cheaper products, faster. . . . The model works. Today more than 35% of our new products in market have elements that originated from outside P&G, up from about 15% in 2000. . . . Through connect and develop—along with improvements in other aspects of innovation related to product cost, design and marketing—our R&D productivity has increased by nearly 60%.[4]

While former CEO Jack Welch leveraged GE's size for innovation, current CEO Jeffrey Immelt is leveraging its diversity by bringing together experts from across its many business units in interdisciplinary task forces to promote innovation. As University of Michigan professor and long-time GE watcher Noel M. Tichy observed, "The cross-business fertilization of research was marginal under Jack Welch, but Jeff has created an excitement and energy around the concept."[5]

1 *Business Week,* "'Mosh Pits' of Creativity" (November 7, 2007), reprint version from businessweek.com.

2 Catherine Holahan, "Yahoo's Bid To Think Small," *Business Week* (February 26, 2007).

3 *Business Week,* "Big Blue Brainstorm," (August 7, 2006), reprint version from businessweek.com.

4 Larry Huston and Nabil Sakkab, "Connect and Develop: Inside Procter & Gamble's New Model for Innovation," *Harvard Business Review* (March 2006), 61.

5 Claudia H. Deutsch, "G.E. Finds Strength In Its Diversity," *New York Times* (February 7, 2007), C8. ▲

Make Room Today for the Future. Organizations determined to make their futures must "make room" for the future in the way they do business today. Resources (that is, people and dollars) must be allocated to the future, organizational space carved out for it; and corporate culture opened to first finding and then exploring new ideas for meeting future demand. CEOs must learn to tolerate what brokerage founder Charles Schwab refers to as "the noble failures" as some of their best people (using dollars that could go to stockholders) experiment with "out of the box" ideas and go down in flames.[24]

Management professor and consultant Gary Hamel describes Silicon Valley, with its open market for ideas, capital and talent as "the distilled essence of entrepreneurial energy" and argues that corporations have to "learn how to bring the energy and ethos of the Valley inside."[25] This is exactly right—organizations have to make room today for the future to "incentivize" innovation.

Empower change agents. A CEO empowers a planner to help an organization define the future demand for its products, services, or capabilities. A CEO also needs to empower change agents to test the validity of new ideas on how to meet that future demand. This is the supply side of the equation. Putting dollars and people against a new idea creates teams that are invested in making the new idea work. The upside rewards for change agents should be high (or they will take their ideas outside to start-up city) and the downside risks low (no one volunteers to test out new ideas in a one-mistake organization). Clayton M Christensen and Michael Overdorf believe that how an organization creates "new organizational space" for innovation depends on how radically the new idea challenges existing organizational values and processes: a new product can be tested by a matrixed team set up inside an organization, but exploring a new line of business may require spinning out or even acquiring a new organization to ensure the idea gets sufficient resources and energy.[26] Developing organizational foresight about future demand is critical, but unless agents are empowered to experiment with different ways of meeting that demand, it is wasted.

Make a decision quickly. In the Net-speed, Early-Bird-Gets-All-the-Worms New Economy, organizations determined to last can't spend a lot of time mulling over the future—they have to get off the pot and decide how they are going to make their futures. *Business Week* believes that the 21st century corporation will have to be fast to survive and cites Intel chairman Andy Grove: "The Internet is a tool, and the biggest impact of that tool is speed. The speed of actions, the speed of deliberations, and the speed of information has increased, and it will continue to increase."[27] Compaq's former chief financial officer told Thomas L. Friedman: "If you're successful at being fast,

Future Making at IBM

The process that IBM used to make its bet on Linux and open source computing is a model case for the precepts of Future Making. As chronicled by *New York Times* reporter Steve Lohr, IBM senior vice president Sam Palmisano learned during an October 1999 global tour [Get Out in the Field] that the preferred language of the young programmers [Talk to the Next Generation] was Linux, a version of the UNIX operating system available free on the Internet.[1] Within days, Nick Bowen, a senior researcher at IBM Watson lab, was made head of the 11-person team [Empower a Change Agent] to figure out quickly (in seven weeks) how the entire company could adapt to Linux.[2] The Bowen report recommended that:

> [IBM] should push Linux as the operating system of choice for the Internet—more robust and reliable than Windows NT and eventually overtaking Solaris, Sun's flavor of UNIX, as the industry standard for UNIX. The goal would be to win the hearts and minds of perhaps the most influential audience in computing—the software developers who write the applications that bring the Web to life and make Internet commerce work."[3]

By Christmas, IBM CEO Louis V. Gerstner Jr. had approved the future-making bet [Make a Decision Quickly] and created a Linux czar responsible for making sure IBM "gets" the Internet [Make It Happen].

---

1 *New York Times* (March 20, 2000), C1.

2 Ibid., C11.

3 Ibid. ▲

---

by definition you'll get big. But if you're just big, and not fast, you're goin' down."[28] Friedman noted that the CFO (and the CEO) went down nine months later "for being a little slow to see the ways the Internet is changing the ways computers are sold and serviced."[29] Future making today is not for the faint-hearted or slow-witted—make decisions quickly.

Innovation, by definition, means change—and change is hard. It's also not free. You have to invest in the future, committing time, people, and dollars to exploring and experimenting with new ideas. And if you are in the technology business, you have to invest even more in future making when times are hard. Even though the 2000–2001 tech crash cut Intel's market valuation by over two thirds, then CEO and President, Craig R. Barrett, was adamant:

> I've only been in the industry 27 years, and I don't know how many cycles we've been through. There's only one thing that we know that is appropriate that works. You know as a fact that technology never slows down, even in a recessionary cycle. So the only thing you can do is to continue to invest in R&D, continue to try to stay in front of the technology curve, continue to invest and bring out new products and new manufacturing technology. The only way you come out of a recession is with new products. . . This is an industry where technology moves forward relentlessly and to stay ahead you have to invest heavily in R&D in good times and in bad times.[30]

Investing in the future is critical, but then you have to decide on what to do. And to make your organization's future, you have to make sure your future-making decision is implemented.

Making the Future Happen

Learning about the future and investing in the future—if that's all that an organization does, it's merely talking about the future. Former GE CEO Jack Welch clearly understands that learning without action is not future making:

> At the heart of [GE's Boundaryless Learning] culture is an understanding that an organization's ability to learn, and translate that learning into action rapidly, is the ultimate business advantage. . . . This Boundaryless Learning Culture killed any view that assumed the "GE way" was the only way or even the best way. The operative assumption today is that someone, somewhere, has a better idea, and the operative compulsion is to find out who has that better idea, learn it, and put it into action—fast.[31]

Organizations making their future must innovate, changing themselves to meet a changing demand for their products, services or capabilities.

Building organizations that last during an era of rapid, discontinuous change requires both improving how well you do what you do today and preparing to do something quite different tomorrow. James Q. Wilson observed in his classic treatise on bureaucracy that organizations readily innovate when it doesn't

▲ **Future making today is not for the faint-hearted or slow-witted—make decisions quickly.**

change the way they do their tasks but find it very difficult when innovation redefines the tasks the organization performs. The United States Air Force, for example, excels at making aircraft that perform better (although not cheaper) but has taken decades to field effective unmanned aerial vehicles (UAVs). The very concept of UAVs was an oxymoron for the Air Force—flight without pilots in an organization dominated by pilots? It's not surprising that the Air Force did not see a requirement for UAVs in the 1970s and 1980s.

As mentioned earlier, Clayton M. Christensen has demonstrated that the very success firms have achieved in dealing with sustaining innovation undercuts their ability to cope with disruptive innovation. Management professors Michael L. Tushman and Charles A. O'Reilly III believe that winning today requires "ambidextrous" managers capable of leading both evolutionary and revolutionary change:

> The real test of leadership, then, is to be able to compete successfully in both the short term through increasing the alignment or fit among strategy, structure, individual competencies, culture, and processes while simultaneously preparing for the inevitable organization revolutions required by shifting innovation streams. The ability to shape innovation streams hinges on an organization's ability to simultaneously engage in . . . both incremental and radical innovation.[32]

Microsoft Knows How Tough It Is to Keep Innovating

Gary Hamel uses Microsoft as a metaphor for innovation stifling as he asks the reader "to imagine that every innovator in the Valley had to go to Bill Gates for funding. Pretty soon everybody in the Valley would be working to extend the Windows franchise. Goodbye to Netscape. Goodbye to the Network Computer. Goodbye to Java and Jini. Goodbye to Palm Pilot. And goodbye to anything else that might challenge Microsoft's current business model."[1]

Microsoft, however, recognized, belatedly to be sure, that it had to change in order to prosper in an Internet-centric future. In May 2000, CEO Steve Ballmer appointed Linda Stone as Microsoft's new vice president of corporate and industry initiatives and described her new job as "core to our effort to evolve our corporate culture without hurting our competitive edge."[2]

In a series of interviews with young former Microsoft execs, Joseph Nocera underscored the challenge Microsoft faced: its best and brightest were leaving because it had become too hard to get new ideas empowered at Microsoft and Microsoft was no longer "the red-hot center:" "Throughout the PC era, Microsoft employees fervently believed that the software giant was *the* place to work if you wanted to matter in computing. They no longer think that."[3] Once Microsoft's youngest vice president (at 31 years), Sam Jadallah says that "Microsoft preserved its entrepreneurial culture longer than any large company I can think of. But, at some point running the ship becomes more important than plotting the path. The culture of risk taking was disappearing rapidly. And the amount of fun I was having was shrinking."[4] Hard to have fun when the future may be passing you by.

Tushman and O'Reilly understand how difficult it is for managers to operate "part of the time in a world of relative stability and incremental change, and part of the time in a world of revolutionary change," citing former Hewlett-Packard CEO Lou Platt: "We have to be willing to cannibalize what we're doing today in order to ensure our leadership in the future. It's counter to human nature but you have to kill your business while it is still working."[33]

Even though Google and Apple were clearly dominating in new Internet-enabled markets, Microsoft had not stopped fighting the good fight. In 2005, Microsoft reorganized itself (collapsing seven business units into three divisions, each led by a "president" with more decision-making authority), as CEO Ballmer said: "We need to improve agility."[5] In July 2006, Ballmer redefined his job as the "full-time champion of innovation" as Microsoft was redefining itself: "We were a desktop company—that's what people thought of us for many years. We're trying to build two new cores, one in online and one in entertainment."[6] *Washington Post* journalist Sara Kehaulani Goo concluded her article with an amusing, but telling, anecdote about a Microsoft exec attempting to demonstrate voice recognition technology:

> "Dear Mom," he said. The program typed, "Dear Aunt." As he tried to delete the mistake, the voice technology wrote a bizarre, nonsensical string of words: "so double the killer delete select all." The crowd roared.[7]

1 Gary Hamel, "Bringing Silicon Valley Inside," *Harvard Business Review* (September–October 1999), 81.

2 Kara Swisher, "Microsoft Appointee: Change Agent or PR Ploy?" *Wall Street Journal* (May 15, 2000), B1.

3 Joseph Nocera, "I Remember Microsoft," *Fortune* (July 10, 2000), 128.

4 Ibid., 124.

5 Steve Lohr, "Microsoft Shuffles Leadership," *New York Times* (September 21, 2005), C1.

6 Sara Kehaulani Goo, "Microsoft Ready to Shift Focus From Desktop," *Washington Post* (July 28, 2006), D1–D2.

7 Ibid., D2. ▲

Being best in class is increasingly the price of doing business in the hypercompetitive New Economy as globalization and the Internet enables consumers to make instant comparisons of the world's products and prices. Preparing to jump into another line of business may be required to survive during an era of rapid, discontinuous change. Do what you do today really well, but be prepared to jump to the Next Big Thing. Making decisions in real time is critical, but decisions, like plans, must be implemented. Decisions don't really matter unless they are followed by actions. Making them matter is the subject of the next chapter.

In a Nutshell

▲ Building organizations that last during a time of rapid, discontinuous change means building companies that innovate. Organizations making their future must innovate, changing themselves to meet a changing demand for their products, services, or capabilities.

▲ Making the future real, giving it taste and texture, creates the basis for making future-oriented decisions. No one takes actions today to prepare for tomorrow unless one feels the presence of future threats and opportunities.

▲ Making room today for the future means allocating resources (that is, people and dollars) to the future, carving out organizational space for future work and opening the corporate culture to first finding and then exploring new ideas for meeting future demand.

▲ In the Net-speed, Early-Bird-Gets-All-the-Worms New Economy, organizations determined to last must make decisions quickly. Empowering change agents to experiment with new ideas for meeting future demand is critical, but wasted if not followed by future-making decisions.

▲ An organization hasn't really learned anything about the future unless it acts on that knowledge—this is the bottom line of future making. While it is actions that count, decisions usually precede them. Planning events are the best time to get future-oriented decisions because that's when the grip of the future is the strongest.

Notes

1 *New York Times*, "From Intel to Health Care and Beyond" (July 30, 2005), reprint from nytimes.com, 2.

2 Arshad Mohammed, "Bowing Out and Letting Go, *New York Times* (May 3, 2006), D5.

3 Clayton M. Christensen, Scott D. Anthony, and Erik A. Roth, *Seeing What's Next: Using the Theories of Innovation to Predict Industry Change* (Boston, MA: Harvard Business School Publishing Corporation, 2004), 293.

4 Ibid., 278–79.

5 Alex Taylor III, "Billion-Dollar Bets," *Fortune* (June 27, 2005), Fortune Archive online version, 2.

6 Thomas A. Stewart, "Growth's Uncharted Road," *Harvard Business Review* (June 2006), 12.

7 *Harvard Business Review,* "Growth as a Process": HBR Interview of Jeffrey Immelt by Thomas A. Stewart (June 2006), 62.

8 Ibid., 62.

9 Ibid., 70.

10 Peter F. Drucker, "What Executives Should Remember," *Harvard Business Review* (February 2006), 149.

11 *Business Week,* "The 21st Century Corporation," editorial (August 28, 2000), 278.

12 Nicholas Stein, "The World's Most Admired Companies," *Fortune* (October 2, 2000), 183.

13 William Drozdiak, "Cisco Looks Across the Pond for Profits," *Washington Post* (February 20, 2001), E4.

14 Clayton M. Christensen and Michael E. Raynor, *The Innovator's Solution: Creating and Sustaining Successful Growth* (Boston, MA: Harvard Business School Press, 2003), 126.

15 Gary Hamel, "Strategy as Revolution" (July–August 1996), 74.

16 Andrew S. Grove, *Only the Paranoid Survive: How to Exploit the Crisis Points that Challenge Every Company* (New York: Currency/Doubleday, 1999), 92–93.

17 Cliff Edwards, "Inside Intel," *Business Week* (January 9, 2006, reprint from businessweek.com).

18 Peter F. Drucker, *Management Challenges for the 21st Century* (New York: Harper-Collins, 1999), 89, 84.

19 Claudia H. Deutsch, "Hot Product Has Corning Thriving and Wary," *New York Times* (September 20, 2005), C1.

20 David Kirkpatrick, "Still Feisty After All These Years," *Fortune* (October 31, 2005), Fortune Archive online reprint version, 1.

21 John F. Welch, "A Company To Be Proud Of," presented at the General Electric Company 1999 Annual Meeting, Cleveland, Ohio, April 21, 1999.

22 Rebecca Buckman, "Pick of the Crop," *Wall Street Journal* (June 1, 2006), B1.

23 Pamela L. Moore with Diane Brady, "Running the House that Jack Built," *Business Week* (October 2, 2000), 130.

24 Nicholas Stein, "The World's Most Admired Companies," *Fortune* (October 2, 2000), 180.

25 Gary Hamel, "Bringing Silicon Valley Inside," *Harvard Business Review* (September–October 1999), 72.

26 Clayton M. Christensen and Michael Overdorf, "Meeting the Challenge of Disruptive Change," *Harvard Business Review* (March–April 2000), 74.

27 John A. Byrne, "Management by Web," *Business Week* (August 28, 2000), 88.

28 Thomas L. Friedman, *The Lexus and the Olive Tree* (New York: Farrar, Straus and Giroux, 1999), 173.

29 Ibid.

30 Seth Schiesel, "Technology Leaders Get Their Bearings," *New York Times* (March 12, 2001), C5.

31 John F. Welch, "A Learning Company and Its Quest for Six Sigma," presented at the General Electric Company 1997 Annual Meeting, Charlotte, NC, April 23, 1997.

32 Michael L. Tushman and Charles A. O'Reilly III, *Winning Through Innovation: A Practical Guide to Leading Organizational Change and Renewal* (Boston, Mass: Harvard Business School Press, 1997), 36–37.

33 Ibid., 36.

6

Making Decisions Matter

IN THIS CHAPTER I argue that visions, plans, and decisions are all just statements of intent. They are the products of planning, but most definitions of planning stop there. From the future-making perspective, however, this is still future talking. *Future making,* whether done informally or formally (in which case, I call it "planning"), *is defined by the **actions** an organization takes today to prepare to meet the future demand for its goods, services, or capabilities.*

Implementing any decision is always harder than making it. Implementing future-making decisions is especially hard because the pains and gains of future making are often separate in time and place. The result may be near-term pain for long-term gain, and who pays the price for investing in the future is rarely the one who gains from the dis-investment in something that is being done today. Resistance comes naturally to today's bill payer for tomorrow.

"Discipline" and "accountability" are terms not usually associated with planning, but they are critical to *serious* future making. A planning process that produces only new investment decisions but no dis-investment decisions is not disciplined. The planner has failed to facilitate the tough decisions, and the CEO has failed to make them; they should be held accountable. Once (or, perhaps, if) tough future-making decisions have been made, everybody must be held accountable for implementing them.*

---

* In a January 2006 Harvard Business Review article ("Who has the D? How Clear Decision Roles Enhance Organizational Performance"), Paul Rogers and Marcia Blenko also emphasize the importance of "making good decisions *(continued on next page)*

The imperative to match actions to words is a constant, perhaps even irritating, theme of this book. In part, no doubt, this reflects my experience in Washington, the world's capital of bloviation, where the gaps between words and deeds are usually chasms. Jeffrey Pfeffer and Robert I. Sutton, however, indicate that the "knowing-doing gap" and the "willingness to let talk substitute for action" are just as common in the business world:

> "Between the conception / and the creation / Falls the Shadow," T.S. Eliot wrote in "The Hollow Men," his great poem about human inertia. In business, that shadow is composed of words. When confronted with a problem, people act as if discussing it, formulating decisions, and hashing out plans for actions are the same thing as actually fixing it. It's an understandable response— after all, talk, unlike action, carries little risk. But it can paralyze a company.[1]

Pfeffer and Sutton, both professors themselves, argue further that management education, because it grades students "on how much they say and how smart they sound in class" rather than (as with pilots or doctors) learning by doing, trains managers (and consultants) in the art of "smart talk," not smart doing.[2] Converting words into actions is always the challenge—and follow-up is critical to meeting this challenge.

It's the Follow-up

At the Pentagon where I once worked, there is an expression in daily conversational use that signifies how monolithic and reflexive the resistance to change is. Anyone proposing change is likely to hear that

---

and making them happen quickly" (pg. 54), but they, in effect, expand the definition of decision making by stating that "good decision making doesn't end with a decision; it ends with implementation." (pg. 59). I think this formulation conflates two very different processes—making decisions, on the one hand, and implementation and execution, on the other—that require very different skills and need to be addressed separately to ensure that both are done. Lack of implementation doesn't mean poor decision making; it just means that good decision making was wasted because it wasn't implemented.

"the building" won't go for it. Not the Defense Department or the agency involved, but, "the building." A former high-level official told me that upon his appointment, it wasn't until his third meeting with his team that "the building" (and you could substitute almost any department) realized that he was *serious* about making a particular change. And that's when deliberate efforts to resist change began, using tactics that ranged from slow rolling (starting to change but at a glacial place) to deliberate non-compliance (calculating that the costs of forcing compliance will be too high for the boss). Not doing what we are supposed to; continuing to do something we shouldn't—it's part of the human condition.

Future making requires follow-up because we are humans, not machines. We find endless ways to rationalize not doing things we're supposed to do, but don't want to do:

▲ Denial is often the first line of defense of change-resisters. I know the boss said to stop doing X, but she didn't really mean it.

  • Cognitive dissonance is a particularly strong form of denial, one that I've experienced but fortunately only in the realm of personal, not business, relationships. Somebody told me to do something, and I promptly forgot about it because it was too unpleasant to contemplate.

▲ Wishful thinking is another favorite. Instead of doing what I'm supposed to do, I'll do something else and maybe that will be good enough.

▲ Procrastination (I'll do it tomorrow, because I have something else I just have to do today) as a way of coping with unpleasant tasks is endemic, because the procrastinator implicitly hopes (more wishful thinking) that the pressure to do something will go away because the boss will forget about it or change her mind.

These are just a few of the cognitive and/or emotional ways that people avoid change. Follow-up is hard work that requires attention and persistence. It's also not fun. The very act of follow-up—that is, closing the loop between decision and action—implicitly questions the good faith and ability of one's colleagues and employees. After all, a decision was made to do something; why shouldn't the CEO just assume it was done? We're all part of the same team, aren't we?

Because decisions matter only if they are translated into action, CEOs, with support from their planners, must follow up to make sure their decisions have effects. However, as the complexity mavens argue, it's a nonlinear world, and actions have both *intended* and *unintended* consequences. Follow-up does double duty: first making sure that decisions produce their intended effects (what I'll call follow-up), then providing a feedback loop to adjust for unintended (usually detrimental) effects (clean up)

It has been my experience that follow-up ("Have you done what you are supposed to do?") requires the most effort. Converting intent into action is always difficult because, as discussed earlier, making sure that decisions matter is about overcoming people's resistance to change. While it's crucial to do, this type of follow-up has a negative aspect mostly because of the emotional response that many people have to their perception that management is looking over their shoulders.

▲ **"Discipline" and "accountability" are terms not usually associated with planning, but they are critical to serious future making.**

Clean up is identifying—and admitting—the unintended effects stemming from a decision—good for everyone—and then revisiting the decision if necessary. Decision makers must be open to changing their course of action because the initial decision may prove to be wrong. One thing is certain: mistakes will be made, as they say. This aspect helps to ensure that adjustments are made as circumstances warrant. But a caution is in order. Those who don't want to do what was decided may try to claim unintended consequences and immediately start the clean up phase as a way of defeating the original decision. Often those seeking to adjust a decision because implementation produced unexpected effects are really decision resisters in another guise.

There is an element to both follow-up and clean-up that needs explicit discussion. This is the need to provide the CEO bad news.

There is no shortage of people who'll tell the boss what a great job he is doing. Positive reinforcement is good, but it's often negative feedback that is really needed, particularly in addressing the words-deeds gap that so often undermines the CEO's efforts. CEOs and their equivalents often "don't want to hear it"—a phrase I've heard too many times to count—but CEOs need to know the bad and the ugly, not just the good, of how others perceive their words and actions. Obviously, this is a tricky role for a planner, and she must play it with respect, restraint, and discretion. But CEOs are just as human as the rest of us—remember, denial ain't just a river in Egypt—and they need to trust someone to tell them when they are straying from their own vision.

Closing the Credibility Gap

It is the follow-up that provides discipline and accountability to future making. By closing the gap between words and deeds, follow-up is also about credibility—we say what we mean and we mean what we say. Follow-up may be the "dark side" of future making, but how effectively it is done separates the future makers from the future talkers. My best practices for follow-up include the following:

Follow-up starts at the top. The CEO or her equivalent sets the tone for the entire organization. The CEO must hold herself accountable for implementing the decisions she has made. In most instances, this means following up with subordinates to ensure that they are implementing decisions. In some cases (for example, an organization's adoption of new ethical standards), the CEO herself must actually do what she said the organization should do. Leading by example really matters, because CEOs lacking the self-discipline to follow *through* (doing what they say they will) or follow *up* (to make sure their decisions are carried out) on their own commitments will erode discipline throughout the organization. There is no follow-up exemption for the top dog, because the pack takes its cue from the leader. CEOs must embrace the role of Enforcer-in-Chief (see Figure 2-1 in Chapter 2).

How Not to Do Follow Up

Although former Secretary of Defense Donald H. Rumsfeld was once widely viewed as the tough, decisive taskmaster who re-established civilian control in the Pentagon, my personal experience was to the contrary. As the lead investigator for a think-tank study on defense, we briefed the Secretary and his top team in March 2004 on the study's phase 1 results. In particular, I told the Secretary that he needed to establish an implementation and execution office that reported to him on how well his decisions were being carried out and that his senior decision-making group should meet bimonthly to review implementation issues, both to promote accountability and organizational learning (by getting feedback directly from those charged with execution). His response was enthusiastic: "By Golly. You're right. We need to do that." At the end of the session, he told both of the senior military officials and a top civilian aide to identify which of the study recommendations they could implement right away and without additional authority.

I followed up a few weeks later and found that the civilian aide had "forgotten" to tell anyone on his staff that there was anything they were supposed to do. After several meetings, the implementation

---

Make the planner the Informer. The CEO needs to be reminded when he—remember, we are all human—and his subordinates fail to implement future-making decisions. The CEO is the judge and jury, but he needs an informer (or, more pejoratively, a tattle-tale or a snitch) to bring potential transgressors to his attention. Of the potential candidates for Future-Making Informer, the planner is the least invested in today's way of doing business and the most invested in the way tomorrow's business should be done. The planner, if empowered by direct access, was there when the decision was made; and, as a facilitator of the decision, he understands the intent of the CEO. Most planners won't embrace the role of Informer—who wants to be a tattle-tale? But the CEO needs someone to tell him when decisions are not being implemented, including when the CEO himself is the transgressor.

process was energized, but then was sidetracked when Secretary Rumsfeld sent a "snowflake" (usually a two to three sentence note from the Secretary to a member of his senior team) to another senior civilian (who hadn't even been at the original meeting) asking about what he was doing to implement our study results, because "there was a lot of good stuff in it." These two senior civilians then got into a turf battle over who the implementer was. In the end, no one ever got back to the Secretary. And he did not follow up.

On the military side, the Joint Staff ran two coordination drills, even though their bosses had already said they were on board, but the majors and colonels found lots of reasons not to carry out any of the recommendations.

At the onset of his second term, the Secretary did set up a tracking system, but it was for tracking responses to his Snowflakes (recipients had so many working hours to acknowledge they had received it, so many days for responding, etc.), not whether his decisions were being implemented. I find this astonishing, since snowflakes, by their very nature, are ephemeral. I was told that by the end of his sixth year, the Secretary generated over 10,000 Snowflakes, an average of thirty per working day. Hard for anyone to get anything done, when inundated by this kind of blizzard. ▲

Put follow-up on the leadership agenda. Any event attended by the CEO and his top team can be a forcing function. If subunits within an organization know that they have to give status-of-implementation reports on previous decisions, they'll do something so that they have something to report. No one likes to tell the boss to his face "no progress." Leadership meetings always have crowded agendas and old business often gets short shrift. But a CEO who carves out space for follow-up is sending an important message to his team: "I care about whether my decisions are being carried out, and I'm holding you personally responsible." Managers who know they personally have to report on follow-up to the boss and in front of their peers will make follow-up a priority. Putting follow-up on the agenda underscores that the bottom line is what is actually done, not what is said.

No identifying problems without the seeds of a solution. Early in my career, I learned an invaluable lesson from a boss who has remained a friend throughout the years. As I entered his office to present him with yet another crisis, before I had even opened my mouth, he slammed his fist down and exclaimed: "Damn it, Clark, you always bring me problems; you never bring me solutions." And that was the last time I ever brought a problem to my boss's attention without also having an idea of what he could do to solve it. Furthermore, it's been my experience along the way that senior managers are more likely to take ownership of a problem if they have some idea of how to solve it. Jeffrey Pfeffer and Robert Sutton report on one reform-oriented manager who "believed that one of the biggest barriers to change was that people constantly whined about things but didn't take responsibility for making them better. She had "No Whining" patches sewn on everybody's uniform and explained that complaining about something without trying to do anything about it was not acceptable."[3] Instituting a rule that no one can bring forward a problem without some idea of how to solve it not only reinforces a bias towards action but also makes follow-up easier.

No decisions without assignments and deadlines. Military organizations know how to execute, since mission execution is at the core of their operational culture. The leadership of the United States Air Force meets three times a year at meetings called "CORONA." Each meeting produces a list of CORONA assignments, or taskers as they are called, that, for each decision, assigns an Office of the Person Responsible (or OPR) for the action and sets a deadline. In this case, implementation begins with *who* is responsible and *when* will it get done—and delegates the *how* it gets done to the responsible office. This approach—assigning task owners—is not unique, but follow-up is about discipline and accountability which are key strengths of military organizations.

Closing the loop between decision and action. It's the follow-up.

Execution—It's All the Rage Now

Execution is getting its due. It is the prism through which we can examine, sharpen, and judge our actions to make the future. And it provides us with a means to tackle the tough job of culture change, as I will discuss later in this chapter.

Former Honeywell International CEO Larry Bossidy and long-time CEO adviser Ram Charan became the new gurus of execution in 2002, when they published *Execution: The Discipline of Getting Things Done.* Formerly defined as the "systematic process of rigorously discussing hows and whats, questioning, tenaciously following through, and ensuring accountability," Bossidy and Charan elevated execution to its proper status:[4]

> Most often today the difference between a company and its competitor is the ability to execute. If your competitors are executing better than you are, they're beating you in the here and now, and the financial markets won't wait to see if your elaborate strategy plays out. So leaders who can't execute don't get free runs anymore. Execution is *the* great unaddressed issue in the business world today.[5]
>
> No strategy delivers results unless it's converted into specific actions.[6]
>
> When companies fail to deliver on their promises the most frequent explanation is that the CEO's strategy was wrong. But the strategy by itself is not often the cause. Strategies most often fail because they aren't executed well. Things that are supposed to happen don't happen.[7]

Bossidy and Charan go on to say that "follow-through is the cornerstone of execution, and every leader who's good at executing follows through religiously:

> Following through ensures that people are doing the things they are committed to, according to the agreed timetable. It exposes any lack of discipline and connection between ideas and action, and forces the specificity that is essential to synchronize the mov-

ing parts of an organization. If people can't execute the plan because of changed circumstances, follow-through ensures they deal swiftly and creatively with new conditions.[8]

While I prefer to say that a CEO must both *follow through* and do what she says she will do and *follow up* to make sure her decisions are carried out, the fundamental point is the same—corporate decisions don't matter unless the CEO *and* her company walk the walk and actually do what they say they will.

Moreover, I share Bossidy and Charan's belief that the ability to execute is a great discriminator. Pfeffer and Sutton quote Richard Kovacevich, CEO of Wells Fargo Bank, one of Jim Collin's good-to-great companies: "I could leave our strategic plan on a plane, and it wouldn't make any difference. No one could execute it. Our success has nothing to do with planning. It has to do with execution."[9] In a *Harvard Business Review* interview, then-CEO of Dell, Kevin Rollins, said when asked why other companies can't "beat you at your own game:"

> The same reason why Kmart can't imitate Wal-Mart. What Wal-Mart does isn't rocket science—it's retailing. Why can't everybody be Wal-Mart or JetBlue or Samsung or whatever the best company in their industry is? Because it takes more than strategy. It takes years of consistent execution for a company to achieve sustainable competitive advantage. So while Dell does have a superior business model, the key to our success is years and years of DNA development within our teams that is not replicable outside the company. Other companies just can't execute as well as we do.[10]

While it is clear that both Wells Fargo and Dell have—or perhaps, had in the case of Dell*—really good business strategies, both Kovacevich and Rollins understate the importance of planning as they place great emphasis on execution. But, as I will discuss in the next chapter, having the right strategy and plan is really important, although not sufficient, for sustained success. Jim Collin's good-to-great companies focused on those business areas in which they could

---

* The limits to Dell's execution strategy is addressed in chapter 7.

be world-class. It's not enough to have a good idea or a good strategy if you can't execute it better than anyone else. Ask Carly Fiorina who was fired as the CEO of Hewlett Packard in February 2005. NCR's Mark Hurd took over and, according to *Business Week*, "admits he's pretty much running her strategy, albeit in a much more focused, disciplined way" and told employees in one of his first plant visits that the reason HP's stock had tanked was "because shareholders don't believe we can do what we say we'll do."[11] Mark Hurd knows that actions speak louder than words—when a *Fortune* interviewer asked him if he needed to articulate a vision, Hurd responded: "Remember [Thomas] Edison's quote: 'Vision without execution is a hallucination.' I have a hard time separating strategy from operations, because they all have to flow together."[12] Under Hurd, HP's stock price had increased by 80 per cent in a year-plus, and HP appeared poised to pass IBM in 2007 as the world's largest IT company. Strategy and planning are about doing the *right* job; execution is about doing the job *right*. You have to do both.

▲ **Strategy and planning are about doing the right job; execution is about doing the job right. You have to do both.**

A Word About Organizational Culture

The bottom line for future making is what an organization actually does to better prepare itself for the future. Having an inspiring vision, developing a good plan, and making the right decisions—all important, but not sufficient. It's the implementation that counts.

Sometimes, the actions needed to prepare for the future are of a nature to require changes in the organization's culture, a process generally regarded as arduous and prone to failure. A full treatment of cultural change is beyond the scope of this book, but Future Reps should take heart—there is a way. At a minimum, CEOs and other top executives must understand their organization's culture. This understanding will tell the CEO if the culture has to change in order to make the organization's future.

▲ ▬▬▬▬▬▬▬▬▬▬▬▬▬▬▬▬▬▬▬▬▬▬▬▬▬

The Poster Child of Execution: IBM's Lou Gerstner

Louis V. Gerstner, Jr., the miracle-worker who resuscitated IBM and made it a dominant player, became infamous when he held his 100-days press conference and, as he later recalled in *Who Says Elephants Can't Dance?* said:

"There's been a lot of speculation as to when I'm going to deliver a vision of IBM, and what I'd like to say to all of you is that the last thing IBM needs right now is a vision."

You could almost hear the reporters blink.

I went on: "What IBM needs right now is a series of very tough-minded, market-driven, highly effective strategies for each of its businesses—strategies that deliver performance in the market-place and shareholder value. And that's what we are working on.

"Now, the number-one priority is to restore the company to profitability. I mean, if you're going to have a vision for a company, the first frame of that vision better be that you're making money and that the company has got its economics correct."[1]

On the day that he became CEO (March 26, 1993), Gerstner told the Corporate Management Board (which he later disbanded as being too bureaucratic) that they needed to "right-size" as quickly as possible, and what he meant by right-size was: 'We have to benchmark our costs versus our competitors and then achieve best-in-class status."[2] During his first hundred days, he made four critical decisions:[3]

▲ "Keep the company together."

[From his prior experience at American Express and RJR Nabisco, he believed IT customers would get tired of trying to bring

Defining—and changing when necessary—the culture of an organization is a huge challenge for the leader. Changing the way people *think* about themselves and how they do their jobs can take a generation, if it's achievable at all. But it is possible to change—and relatively quickly—how people *behave* in their jobs. To some extent, it is a chicken-and-egg problem: Is a shared mental model or value set or culture the necessary precursor to unified action? Or is it better

all the different products together and would want a large, integrated company that could do it for them.]

▲ "Change our fundamental economic model."

[Discovering that IBM was spending 42 cents to produce $1 of revenue while its competitors were spending 31 cents, Gerstner launched a "massive program of expense reduction" as a "matter of survival, not choice."]

▲ "Reengineer how we did business."

[Although "reengineering is difficult, boring and painful," Gerstner knew that IBM's processes were "cumbersome and highly expensive" and had to be fundamentally changed.]

▲ "Sell underproductive assets in order to raise cash."

[Noting that "only a handful of people understand how precariously close IBM came to running out of cash in 1993," Gerstner sold its U.S. government business, its New York City headquarters, and its fine-art collection. He continued to streamline the company, but "for a different purpose: focus."]

Gerstner knew that IBM didn't need a new vision or some bold strategic initiative: "The real issue was going out and making things happen every day in the marketplace. Our products weren't bad; our people were good people; our customers had long, successful relationships with us. We just weren't getting the job done. . . . Fixing IBM was all about execution."[4]

1 Gerstner, *Who Says Elephants Can't Dance? Inside IBM's Historic Turnaround* (New York: HarperBusiness/HarperCollins Publishers, 2002), 68–69.
2 Ibid., 22.
3 Ibid., 57–67.
4 Ibid., 71. ▲

to bypass how people think and focus directly on how people perform their jobs?

There is no question that how people *think* about their jobs affects how they *perform* their jobs. Values and beliefs are important. CEOs, however, are not observers of culture but changers of culture. In a March 2005 *Harvard Business Review* interview, Kevin Rollins described an initiative to grow more leaders internally at Dell: "Our senior managers are measured and compensated on it [developing people]. If we'd put in place a program without metrics, no one would have taken it seriously."[13] Of course, it's not just performance metrics; it's also performance-based compensation. As Bossidy and Charan state with no qualification, "the foundation of changing behavior is linking rewards to performance and making the linkages transparent. . . . If a company rewards and promotes people for execution, its culture will change."[14] This point is echoed by the all-purpose management guru, Gary Hamel, who believes that "blaming organizational underperformance on culture is something of a cop out. To change corporate culture, organizations need to change the management systems that define, reinforce and reward management behaviors."[15]

The message, I think, is clear—change the behavior of your employees and their minds will follow. CEOs trying to create or change an organization's culture should focus on behavior. Changing the way people *think* about themselves and their jobs is too hard and takes too long. It's easier and quicker to change how people *behave* in their jobs by setting performance standards and enforcing them.

Doing the Follow-Up Walk

Follow-up. Closing the loop. Making sure it gets done. Simple injunctions, to be sure, but critical to making decisions matter. Execution clearly counts in the New Economy.

The deeply troubled U.S. automobile industry has sought IBM-like turnarounds by seeking to emulate the Gerstner execution model. When Ford chairman and family scion Bill Ford brought in Boeing's Alan R. Mulally to replace him as CEO, Ford told his employees: "Alan knows what it's like to have your back to the wall—and fight your way out with a well-conceived plan and great execution."[16] Although, according to *Fortune,* General Motors CEO Richard Wagoner is under growing pressure "to swing for the fences" by making a "bold commitment to hybrid cars or fuel cells, pull off a merger [or] precipitate a showdown with the unions," Wagoner "prefers a methodical approach, convinced that better execution on all the critical fronts—cost, quality, product development, marketing—is what will save GM."[17] In a telling concession, Wagoner admits that GM must solve its credibility problem first: "We've been around way too long, and people have heard all our lies [about quality, performance and durability]. We just have to deliver."[18]

Follow-up is about returning to basics. The Grandfather of management gurus, Peter F. Drucker, states it plainly: "Management must focus on the results and performance of the organization" and the first task of management is "to define what results and performance are in a given organization."[19] It's not what we say we do; it's what we do that matters. Follow-up makes decisions matter. It separates the future makers from the future talkers.

In a Nutshell

▲ Future making is defined by the *actions* an organization takes today to prepare to meet the future demand for its goods, services, or capabilities. Future-making plans are good, and future-making decisions are critical, but it's the actions that separate future makers from future talkers.

▲ Implementing future-making decisions is hard because the pains and gains of future making are separate in time and place—it's near-term pain for long-term gain and who pays is not usually who gains.

▲ Follow-up is not fun. The act of follow-up —closing the loop between decision and action—implicitly questions the good faith and ability of one's colleagues and employees. Follow-up means asking someone if they did what they were supposed to do.

▲ There is clean-up as well as follow-up. Clean-up acknowledges when plans have not worked, or have brought unintended consequences, and it fixes them.

▲ Follow-up starts at the top. CEOs lacking the self-discipline to do what they say they will erode discipline throughout the organization. If a CEO doesn't care enough about making her decisions matter to do follow-up, his subordinates won't either.

▲ When making a decision, assign responsibility for implementing it and set deadlines for making it happen. To the extent possible, decisions should be self-executing. Performance is the bottom line.

Notes

1 Jeffrey Pfeffer and Robert I. Sutton, "The Smart-Talk Trap," *Harvard Business Review* (May–June 1999), 136.

2 Ibid., 137.

3 Ibid., 142.

4 Larry Bossidy and Ram Charan, *Execution: The Discipline of Getting Things Done* (New York: Crown Business, 2002), 22.

5 Ibid., 5.

6 Ibid., 9.

7 Ibid., 15.

8 Ibid., 127.

9 Jeffrey Pfeffer and Robert I. Sutton, *Hard Facts, Dangerous Half-Truths & Total Nonsense: Profiting from Evidence-Based Management* (Harvard Business School Press, 2006), 145.

10 Thomas A. Stewart and Louise O'Brien, "Execution Without Excuses: An Interview with Michael Dell and Kevin Rollins," *Harvard Business Review* (March 2005), online reprint version, 1–2.

11 Peter Burrows, "Controlling the Damage at HP," *Business Week* (October, 9, 2006), 40.

12 Adam Lashinsky, "Mark Hurd Takes his First Swing at HP," *Fortune* (August 8, 2005) Fortune Archive online version, 3.

13 Stewart and O'Brien, "Execution Without Excuses," 10.

14 Bossidy and Charan, *Execution*, 92.

15 Gary Hamel, Letters to the Editor, *Harvard Business Review* [Hamel responds to letters on his prior article on management innovation] (June 2006), 140.

16 Deborah Stead, ed., Up Front, *Business Week* (September 18, 2006), 99.

17 Alex Taylor III, "Can One Man Save GM?" *Fortune* (September 19, 2005) Fortune Archive online version, 2.

18 Ibid.

19 Peter F. Drucker, *Management Challenges for the 21st Century* (New York: Harper-Collins Publishers, Inc., 1999), 39.

7

Choosing the Right Strategy

ALTHOUGH MOST BOOKS of this genre begin with strategy, *Future Making* saves strategy to the end. In part, this reflects my own bias as an "idea guy" in Washington, which has far, far more talkers than doers, which led me to value the ability to make ideas happen and to convert words to actions. Even though I continue to believe that coming up with strategies is a lot easier than executing them, having the right strategy matters, because flawless execution of a bad strategy, as any student of military history knows, just brings defeat faster. Of course, choosing the right strategy matters, but I believe real future making requires a different way of thinking about strategy.

Execution-as-Strategy

As discussed in the previous chapter, former CEO Lou Gerstner's strategy for digging IBM out of its hole was execution, a model that many current CEOs are emulating. For example, when Mark Hurd took over Hewlett Packard after Carly Fiorina (a first-tier "idea guy" if there ever was one) was fired as CEO, he, according to the *Wall Street Journal*'s Michael S. Malone, "returned H-P to what he calls the basic 'blocking and tackling' of getting products out on time, improving quality and service, and increasing profit margins."[1] It's a truism, to be sure, but improving execution is always the answer when the problem is poor execution, since it both improves the bottom line and makes it harder for competitors to steal good ideas that are poorly executed. As someone who has extensive U.S. government experience, I know that the value of operational effectiveness and efficiency should not be underestimated.

But, as with anything, there are limits to execution as a strategy, because competitors can steal both good ideas and good management practices. The guru of competition, Michael Porter, has never believed that execution excellence provides a sustainable advantage because "best practice competition eventually leads to competitive convergence," which now happens faster in the Information Age:

> The Internet is arguably the most powerful tool available for enhancing operational effectiveness. By easing and speeding the exchange of real-time information, it enables improvements throughout the entire value chain, across almost every company and industry. And because it is an open platform with common standards, companies can often tap into its benefits with much less investment than was required to capitalize on past generations of information technology.[2]

For Clayton Christensen, the central question of innovation is how it is executed—as sustaining or disruptive innovation. Disruptive innovation puts cheaper products in at the low end of the market and then moves up market in a way that eventually dooms those engaged in sustaining innovation. He offers the example of disk drive manufacturers that engaged in sustaining innovation—improving their product—and saw their margins consumed by commoditization of the product:

> Here's a frightening example: The first one-gigabyte 3.5-inch disk drives were introduced to the world in 1992 at prices that enable their manufacturers to earn 60 percent gross margins. These days, disk drive companies are struggling to eke out 15 percent margins on drives that are sixty times better [and capable of storing and retrieving data in circular tracks that are only 0.00008 inch apart on the disk surface]. . . . And yet disk drives of this genre are regarded today as undifferentiable commodities.[3]

It's no wonder that IBM (and many others) got out of the PC business.

Dell's Execution-Focused Business Model May Have Run Its Course

In a little over a year since Michael Dell and Kevin Rollins gave their "real men execute" interview to *Harvard Business Review* (see Chapter 6), Dell's numbers first slowed and then stagnated in mid-2006. At first, Dell stoutly defended Rollins and acknowledged mistakes (such as outsourcing a lot of their customer service to India and Pakistan, which led to declining repeat business) because they had been "managing cost instead of managing service and quality."[1] Kevin Rollins, however, was gone as CEO on January 31, 2007, as Michael Dell stated: "I'm not hiring a COO or a CEO. I'm going to be the CEO for the next several years. We're going to fix this business."[2]

Clayton Christensen, however, had visited Dell and Rollins in 1998 and 2000 and warned them, according to *Business Week,* that "they needed to focus on growth five to eight years out, on the model that would augment their built-to-order machines."[3] In noting that "long-term success demands constant reinvention," *Business Week* also quoted Jim Mackey, an expert on large-company growth:

> Dell is a textbook example of single-formula growth: "We make PCs cheap. This is what we do, and we do it a lot." You can grow very fast when you're on a single formula, but when you get to a certain point [$50 billion in revenues, about $10 billion less than Dell's 2006 revenues], you don't have the ability to create new growth.[4]

Michael Dell, however, says, "I do think that Dell's core strengths historically will be its core strengths in the future."[5] Denial ain't just a river in Egypt.

---

1 David Kirkpatrick, "Dell in the Penalty Box," *Fortune* (September 5, 2006), Fortune Archive reprint version, 3.

2 Louise Lee and Peter Burrows, "Is Dell Too Big for Michael Dell?" *Business Week* (February 12, 2007), 33.

3 Nanette Byrnes and Peter Burrows, "Where Dell Went Wrong," *Business Week* (February 19, 2007), 62.

4 Ibid.

5 Ibid., 63. ▲

Execution is critical, in my view, and, under some circumstances works as a strategy. London Business School professor Donald N. Sull argues that "in unpredictable markets, execution is strategic. Operational improvements keep companies in the game. Firms that maintain the pressure [to be operationally efficient] during lulls can outlast less efficient rivals when sudden-death threats descend and can capitalize on golden opportunities beyond the reach of lesser firms."[4] But any strategy, like any idea, can be copied, and some leaner, more efficient competitor eventually will. Execution is necessary, but never sufficient in the long run.

Innovation-as-Strategy

As discussed in Chapter 5, the imperative to innovate has become even stronger in the Information Age. During a time of rapid, discontinuous change, organizations that don't change, by definition, become obsolete. Adrian J. Slywotsky, vice president of Mercer Management Consulting, Inc., told *The Washington Post* that the "innovation cycle is so fast that it takes only a matter of months before competitors come up with me-too products" that compete with them in a retail market dominated by large chains (see Wal-Mart) that have driven prices so low in the electronics business that profits come largely from installation fees and warranties."[5] Former IBM CEO Lou Gerstner noted early in his tenure that the "whole Silicon Valley ethos—lightening speed to market with just-good-enough products—wasn't simply foreign to IBM, it was an entirely new game."[6]

IBM subsequently decided to escape the commoditization trap by joining the open source movement and giving away software and services that it had previously charged for. In a 2005 e-mail to *Fortune,* IBM CEO Sam Palmisano claimed that his "openness" strategy was a "spur to innovation itself" because it "will make the pie bigger" by stimulating growth. He went on to say: "This isn't theory for us. Collaborative innovation today is crucial to every aspect of our business. We've learned how to deliver value within this kind of business system and how to make money."[7] *Fortune*'s David Kirkpatrick noted, however, that both IBM and IBM watchers know "that openness is a great strategy only so long as you keep inventing products that let you take advantage of the doors you've opened."[8] In addition, innovation increasingly is the means by which big firms grow bigger—as GE CEO Jeffrey Immelt told *Fortune:* "We don't buy growth, we grow what we buy."[9] And the key to "organic growth"—that is, increased sales or return on business units already part of the company—is innovation. All must innovate, all the time.

So, if innovation, like execution, is a must-do for 21st century organizations, is it really a strategy? Or, conversely, are non-innovation or poor-execution strategies as well? Certainly, no organization deliberately embraces poor performance as a means to making profits or achieving its stated purpose. Larry Bossidy and Ram Charan, our apostles of execution, argue that a "good strategic planning process also requires the utmost attention to the *hows* of executing the strategy" and that strategies that do not "address the hows" will fail.[10]

At first, I thought that these execution-as-strategy advocates had misunderstood the meaning of strategy, which, after all, is *how* one uses the means at one's disposal to achieve some end. I then realized that if execution and innovation, much like growth, are necessary means to staying profitable in the 21st century, the key issue is not whether you execute or innovate, but how do you do it. The how-issues were addressed in earlier chapters; the question here is: how does an innovative, high-performance company decide what to do? If you can't innovate or execute, you *really* have problems, but if you can, you still need to decide what to do. At the end of his first year of using execution-as-strategy for leading IBM out of its near-death experience, Lou Gerstner realized that "what lay ahead—devising a strategy for a fundamental new world and reinventing an encrusted culture from the DNA out" were challenges of "a vastly different order."[11]

▲ **Choosing the right strategy matters, but I believe real future making requires a different way of thinking about strategy.**

How to Think about Strategy

Accenture's managing director of the strategy practice, Walter Shill, says that "being strategic today is like being a white water rafter. You have to react immediately to opportunities or moves by a competitor—or risk being overtaken."[12] This doesn't sound very strategic, since strategy is about taking purposeful actions in the pursuit of some objective. Acting like a white water rafter seems very inconsistent with Jim Collins' good-to-great companies and their "Hedgehog Concepts" (see Chapter 4)—the "simple, crystalline concepts" that synthesize a company's understanding of the market and what it can excel at and provides a "simple, yet deeply insightful, frame of reference for all decisions."[13] After all, who ever hear of a hedgehog on a raft?

Not surprisingly, Michael Porter, the authority on competitiveness, has the answer to this seeming contradiction. He notes that all companies want to maximize return on investment and all want to do so by creating a "sustainable competitive advantage."[14] Porter argues that there are two levels of strategy—a "basic" strategy that expresses the essence of a company's business model and a constantly changing strategy for how that basic strategy is executed in a changing environment. His examination of sustained, high-performance companies (which included many of the good-to-great companies that Jim Collins studied) reveals a "consistency of basic strategy combined with relentless improvement in the ways they implement them."[15]

In applying Porter's construct in my own writings on the practice of national security strategy, I used the terms "grand strategy" and "strategy" to differentiate between a nation's underlying strategic concept and its strategies for implementing it.[16] If I were a classic military planner, I would use "strategy" and "tactics," but most consultants who provide advice on corporate strategy undoubtedly believe their influence goes beyond the tactical. If I were still in the Pentagon, I might distinguish between "Big S" Strategy and "small s" strategy, but fortunately this fondness for acronym-play hasn't spilled over into the private sector. I was going to differentiate between a company's "business model" and its "strategy," until *Harvard Business*

Microsoft Gets Disruptive Innovation

In what *New York Times* journalist Steve Lohr characterized as "Internet, Round 2" [Round 1 being Netscape's Internet browser in the mid-1990s], Microsoft is facing off with Google for who will dominate in a new era of free software and high-speed Internet access.[1] In early 2005, Microsoft founder and Chairman Bill Gates brought in Ray Ozzie (and his company) to be his chief technical officer. Ozzie had led the team that created Lotus Notes and founded Groove Networks "to make advanced collaboration software using Internet peer-to-peer technology."[2]

After immersing himself in how Microsoft did business, Ozzie formulated a plan for how Microsoft could meet the challenge posed by a "set of very strong and determined competitors . . . laser-focused on Internet services and service-enabled software" in a memo entitled "The Internet Services Disruption," which was first distributed to senior managers and engineers but then posted on the company's website. In this memo, Ozzie laid out a strategy for how Microsoft must change and stated: "It's clear that if we fail to do so, our business as we know it is at risk. We must respond quickly and decisively."[3]

In a covering note to the Ozzie memo, Gates noted that he had written a memo in 1995 entitled "The Internet Tidal Wave" which drew similar conclusions: "This coming 'services wave' will be very disruptive. The next sea change is upon us."[4] Although Google was still doing extremely well six months later (in mid-2006, as well as today a year later), Gates said that Microsoft would catch up and observed that "this is a rare case where we are being underestimated."[5] Given the fact that Microsoft had over four times as much cash on hand as Google did ($35 billion compared to $8 billion),[6] betting that Microsoft would survive Internet, Round 2 seems like a safe bet.

---

1 Steve Lohr, "Can This Man Reprogram Microsoft?" *New York Times* (December 11, 2005), Section 3, 1.

2 Ibid., 4.

3 Ibid.

4 Ibid.

5 Steve Lohr, "And in This Corner. . .Microsoft and Google Grapple for Supremacy as Stakes Escalate," *New York Times* (May 10, 2006), C14.

6 Ibid. ▲

Review told me that "no one ever defined the term [business model] precisely—it seemed to mean either 'what we do' or 'how we hope to make money someday'—but it always got tossed into conversations about new economy businesses. For a while last year, it supplanted 'business strategy' as the guiding principle for executives and entrepreneurs, justifying a rather cavalier attitude toward profitability and competitive advantage."[17]

There is a way out of this thicket that provides a useful guide on how to think about strategy that allows us to capture both the basic, enduring element of strategy and still survive Shill's white water. I would like to differentiate between an organization's *strategic concept* and the many *strategies* that it adopts in applying that concept to changing circumstances.

An organization's strategic concept provides the context in which it decides upon which strategy (or strategies) to pursue in the face of today's (and tomorrow's) circumstances. When Michael Porter says (see Chapter 4) that "having a strategy is a matter of discipline" and that companies need to stay with it no matter how the market changes, he is talking about a company's strategic concept (which he earlier called "basic strategy"). When Clayton Christensen and Michael Raynor say that "strategy is never static" and that companies must change to survive, they are talking about the strategies that a company must pursue as markets mature and collapse.[18] Jim Collins believes that the good-to-great companies achieved breakthrough results by a "series of good decisions, diligently executed and accumulated one on top of another" and they did this "by infus[ing] the entire process [of deciding what *strategy* to follow at any one time] with the brutal facts of reality" (see Chapter 3) and making those decisions with the "frame of reference" provided by the Hedgehog Concept (also known as the *strategic concept*).[19] In recommending that companies keep their strategies "simple" and "concrete," Michael C. Mankins and Richard Steele quote Bob Diamond, CEO of Barclay Capital:

> We've been very clear about what we will and will not do. We knew we weren't going to go head-to-head with U.S. bulge bracket

firms. We communicated that we wouldn't compete in this way and that we wouldn't play in unprofitable segments within the equity markets but instead would invest to position ourselves for the euro, the burgeoning need for fixed income, and the end of Glass-Steigel. By ensuring everyone knew the strategy [aka *strategic concept*] and how it was different, we've been able to spend more time on tasks [aka *strategies*] that are key to executing this strategy.[20]

The words change, but the underlying message is the same—organizations must really understand their basic approach for doing business, but they need to be very adaptable on how they do it in any particular circumstance.

If surviving in the Internet Era requires world-class execution and innovation capabilities, successful firms need to execute and innovate, no matter what their strategic concept is, in part because it positions them to seize opportunities when they present themselves. In making their case that corporations overstate the importance of strategy, Jeffrey Pfeffer and Robert Sutton note:

> Attributing Intel's success to its own strategic decisions is, however, at least partly incorrect. According to Craig Barrett, the company's former CEO and current chairman, Intel was given the chance to move into microprocessors largely as a result of a strategic decision by IBM to outsource the manufacture of microprocessors for the IBM PC, a lucky break that Intel was smart enough to capitalize on but that had little to do with any planning, rational analysis, or strategy formation by Intel's senior team [which, of course, included Andy Grove, my favorite practitioner-strategist].[21]

London Business School professor Donald Sull imports the "fog of war" from the military lexicon to describe today's "fog of the future" in which firms have sharply limited visibility in volatile markets, and recommends a strategy of "active waiting" by preparing to seize "golden opportunities" (see IBM's decision to outsource production of microprocessors) and cope with "sudden-death threats" (see Intel and the commoditization of the memory chip).[22] To import two additional terms from the military lexicon, Internet Era organizations have to be *operationally ready*—that is, capable today of executing missions—and *strategically responsive*—that is, able to react agilely and effectively to new challenges. In Pentagonese, the abilities to execute and innovate are "critical enablers" and necessary for the success of any organization's strategic concept.

So, a reader might well ask at this point, I understand that two of my strategies have to be innovation and execution, but how do I choose the *right* strategic concept? After all, the title of this chapter is "choosing the right strategy." My first response is a little unresponsive—the *right* strategy, according to this construct, is one that is responsive to evolving circumstances and is in accord with your strategic concept. The reply from an increasingly exasperated reader—No, I asked how one knows when the *strategic concept* is right. There is no good answer to this, as Jim Collins found in interviews with Lyle Everingham and Jim Herring, CEOs of Kroger when it became a good-to-great company:

> [They] were polite and helpful, but a bit exasperated by our questions. To them, it just seemed so clear. When we asked Everingham to allocate one hundred points across the top five factors in the transition [from good to great], he said: "I find your question a bit perplexing. Basically, we did extensive research, and the data came back loud and clear: The supercombination stores were the wave of the future. We also learned that you had to be number one or number two in each market, or you had to exit. Sure, there was some skepticism at first. But once we looked at the facts, there was really no question about what we had to do. So we just did it."[23]

Of course, as we know, "just doing it" is hardly a simple matter, because it often involves changing an organization's culture. But, as stated in Chapter 1, future making begins with making the best effort to understand what the future will demand and deciding what end-states your organization must achieve to be successful, and then acting decisively to move toward those end-states. If you do due diligence and are honest about your situation and yourself, the chances of your finding the *right strategic concept* improve, but, since you are human, there's no guarantee. You had better empower a second-guesser (also known as a planner) to help you discover when (not if) you are wrong.

A Planner's Perspective— Both Dispassionate and Independent

Jim Collins found that it took about four years for the good-to-great company to develop their Hedgehog Concept because getting one was "*an inherently iterative process,* not an event."[24] In making their case for strategic resilience (see Chapter 3), Gary Hamel and Liisa Valikangas believe that organizations must "face up to the inevitability of strategy decay," because strategies can be *replicated* by others, *supplanted* by better strategies, *exhausted* when markets are saturated, and *eviscerated* when something (like the internet) changes everything.[25] If it takes time to build your strategic concept and your strategies change all the time (except for execution and innovation), how do you ensure that you get the feedback you need to take corrective action? Not surprisingly, I believe you need to empower a planner and give her a seat at your decision-making table.

In Chapter 2, I argued that every CEO needs someone, whom I call a "planner," who is not invested in how the organization does business today and can be dispassionate about defining the future demand for an organizations goods, services, or capabilities. This planner should bring an external focus to the table and get out into the field and talk to customers and the next generation. Above all, future-making CEOs need realistic feedback (see Chapter 2's textbox on the importance of realism) to ensure that he and his top team aren't drinking their own bath water and that they get the feedback they need both to refine their strategic concept and to change their strategies. Giving your planner the resources, access, and independence she needs to do the feedback job will help you learn when you are making a mistake and help you be strategically responsive in an era of tumultuous change.

In a Nutshell

▲ Executing strategies is, I believe, more difficult than devising one, but having the right strategy matters, because flawlessly executing the wrong strategy just digs the hole deeper.

▲ Improving execution is always the answer when the problem is poor execution, since it both improves the bottom line and makes it harder for competitors to steal good ideas that are poorly executed. But good execution practices can also be copied, so advantages in operational effectiveness and efficiency are likely to be short-lived, particularly today because the Internet makes it easier and cheaper to copy the leader.

▲ In the Internet Era, it's all innovation, all the time. Markets change so rapidly and information flows so quickly, that private sector firms that don't innovate, don't survive. Organizations not subject to the discipline of the marketplace may survive without innovating, but they'll lose relevance. When the times are a-changing, to paraphrase Bob Dylan, you have to change with them.

▲ An organization's *strategic concept* provides the context in which it decides upon which *strategy* (or strategies) to pursue in the face of today's (and tomorrow's) circumstances. Although leading corporate strategists use different words, the underlying message is the same—organizations must really understand their basic approach for doing business, but they need to be very adaptable on how they do it in any particular circumstance.

▲ If you do due diligence and are honest about your situation and yourself, the chances of your finding the *right strategic concept* improve, but, since you are human, there's no guarantee. That's why a CEO needs a dispassionate, externally-focused, independent planner who provides realistic feedback to help refine the organization's strategic concept and change its strategies to meet changing circumstances.

Notes

1 Michael S. Malone, "The Un-Carly," *Wall Street Journal* (April 14–15, 2007), A9.

2 Michael E. Porter, "Strategy and the Internet," *Harvard Business Review* (March 2001), online reprint version, 9.

3 Clayton Christensen and Michael E. Raynor, *The Innovator's Solution: Creating and Sustaining Successful Growth* (Boston, MA: Harvard Business School Publishing Corp., 2003), 149.

4 Donald N. Sull, "Strategy as Active Waiting," *Harvard Business Review* (September 2005), online reprint version, 7.

5 Steven Pearlstein, "Industries Stuck in Failure Mode," *Washington Post* (January 5, 2003), A10.

6 Louis V. Gerstner, Jr., *Who Says Elephants Can't Dance: Inside IBM's Historic Turnaround* (New York: HarperCollins Publishers, Inc., 2002), 105.

7 David Kirkpatrick, "IBM Shares Its Secrets," *Fortune* (September 5, 2005), Fortune Archive online version, 3.

8 Ibid., 4.

9 Geoffrey Colvin, "The Bionic Manager," *Fortune* (September 19, 2005), Fortune Archive online version, 3.

10 Larry Bossidy and Ram Charan, *Execution: The Discipline of Getting Things Done* (New York: Crown Business, 2002), 178–179.

11 Gerstner, *Who Says Elephants*, 105.

12 Carol Hymowitz, "Two More CEO Ousters Underscore the Need for Better Strategizing," *Wall Street Journal* (September 11, 2006), B1.

13 Jim Collins, *Good to Great* (New York: HarperBusiness, HarperCollins Publishers, Inc., 2001), 95, 70.

14 Michael E. Porter, "Competitive Strategy Revisited: A View from the 1990s," in Paula Barker Duffy, ed., *The Relevance of a Decade: Essays to Mark the First Ten Years of the Harvard Business School Press* (Boston, MA: Harvard Business School Press, 1994), 260.

15 Ibid.

16 Clark A. Murdock, principal author, *Improving the Practice of National Security Strategy: A New Approach for the Post–Cold War World* (Washington, DC: The CSIS Press, 2004), 13.

17 *Harvard Business Review*, "The 2001 HBR List: Breakthrough Ideas for Today's Business Agenda," (April 2001), online reprint version, 2.

18 Christensen and Raynor, *The Innovator's Solution,* 220.

19 Collins, *Good to Great,* 69.

20 Michael C. Mankins and Richard Steele, "Turning Great Strategy into Great Performance," *Harvard Business Review* (July–August 2005), online reprint version, 5.

21 Jeffrey Pfeffer and Robert I. Sutton, *Hard Facts, Dangerous Half-Truths & Total Nonsense: Profiting from Evidence-Based Management* (Boston, MA: Harvard Business School Press, 2006), 143.

22 Sull, "Strategy as Active Waiting," 1–3.

23 Collins, *Good to Great,* 68–69.

24 Ibid., 114.

25 Gary Hamel and Liisa Valikangas, "The Quest for Resilience," *Harvard Business Review* (September 2003), online reprint version, 5.

8

Final Thoughts

Organizations determined to last during an era of rapid change must make their futures happen or risk being overtaken by the future. What works today likely won't work tomorrow. Today's pace of change—fast, discontinuous and broad—leaves little opportunity for successful incrementalism or evolutionary adaptation. Future making is for organizations that are willing to take difficult steps today to better position themselves to survive tomorrow.

There are four steps to future making. They are easy to list, but difficult to undertake. They are:

1. Define—dispassionately—the future demand for the organization's products, services, or capabilities.

2. Determine what end states the organization must achieve in order to be successful in the future.

3. Decide what to start doing today and what to stop doing to better prepare for the future.

4. Do what you say you are going to do.

This is future making. The burden of this book has been to show you how you can be successful at the steps.

Much organizational future making takes place *informally*—crises emerge, the CEO huddles with top management, and decisions are made that have strategic implications for the organization. But future making that relies entirely on informal processes tends to be ad hoc, episodic, often uninformed, and too tightly tied to the present.

Today's leaders are too invested in today's way of doing business, and their definition of future demand will be biased by the all-too-human need to make the future safe for the way they do things today.

When organizations engage *formally* in future making, it is usually called planning. Planning, from this perspective, is the formal process by which an organization takes actions today to prepare to meet the future demand for its goods, services, or capabilities. Planning processes often produce strategic visions and strategic plans, but if they don't result in tough decisions by the senior leadership on what an organization should do today to better prepare itself for the future, they have failed the future-making test. And since visions, plans, and decisions are all statements of intent, they must be acted upon. Otherwise, it's just talking about the future, not future making.

Organizations that can't execute and innovate will struggle in the Internet Era, because information flows so rapidly that good strategies and ideas that are poorly executed will quickly attract more capable imitators. And even good strategies well executed will attract low-end competitors as industries mature, and firms move up the value chain in an effort to sustain profit margins. Information-age organizations must both execute and innovate to survive, regardless of what other strategy they follow.

Organizations need a strategic concept as defined in the previous chapter to provide a context for making decisions on which strategies to pursue in the face of changing circumstances. Being disciplined about adhering to one's basic approach for doing business while at the same time being flexible and adaptable requires a duality that is best captured in advice given by Frederick P. Brooks, Jr., the legendary author of *The Mythical Man-Month: Essays on Software Engineering,* often referred to as the bible of software engineering:

> The best single advice [for a young manager] is a motto I read on the ceiling of a German drinking fraternity in Heidelberg—this cave had been there, I guess, since the 16th century. It said, Numquam incertus; semper apertus: "Never uncertain, always open." Sometimes the first is put as saying, "You can't steer a ship that's not underway." At any given time, you ought to have pretty

clear goals, and know where you're going, and be going there. On the other hand, you always should be open to saying, "Is that what we really ought to be doing? Here's another idea." But sitting still in the water waiting to decide which way to go is the wrong thing to do.[1]

Maintaining this kind of duality is difficult for any one of us. I like to say about myself that I'm remarkably open-minded for someone with such strong opinions, but I'm sure my colleagues, not to mention my wife, think I'm just kidding myself. Most CEOs are too successful, too busy, and too committed to making things happen today to step outside of themselves and dispassionately look at themselves and what they do. That's why they need planners.

For the CEO, Some Final Counsel

Building a firm, company, or organization that lasts in this era of rapid, discontinuous change can be your most enduring legacy. For your organization to prosper tomorrow means much more than doing what you do today better, faster, or cheaper. The very success you enjoy today can be the biggest impediment to change. If you become too psychologically attached to the products and capabilities that have served you so well so far, you may be unable to respond to the disruptive technologies that may be redefining your industry.

Only you can get your organization ready for what's next. Creating a vision for where your organization needs to go, making the strategic decisions that start moving your organization in the right direction, making sure that the decisions are implemented, changing your organization's culture—it all starts at the top. You are the future maker for your organization.

Yours can be an in-box-dominated job. There is no end to the demands on your time; no end to the daily crises that need your attention. The decisions you make or fail to make implicitly determine how well your organization copes with today's change and uncertainty. You try, of course, to "keep the future in mind" as you deal with today's challenges. But can you really be dispassionate enough to question how well today's way of doing business will fit future demand? Are you and your top team taking enough "time outs" from your in-boxes to get your heads into the future?

Establishing a formal, but simple, planning process can help. Your organization can't successfully make its future unless it makes time for future making. Planning events—off-sites, vision summits, planning sessions, and so on—carve out organizational space for you to learn about the future, to make future-oriented decisions, and to ensure that past decisions are followed up by appropriate actions. Only you can give the future a seat at your organization's tables.

Empowering a planner can also help. Your planner can bring a dispassionate, future-oriented perspective to bear on today's decisions. But he or she needs *direct* access to you for that to happen. You need someone who knows you and knows your job, but is not invested in how you are doing your job. Your bet on the future could be wrong. You need a second-guesser in your inner circle—someone whose job it is to raise those uncomfortable "But, sir" or What if" questions—because it's often too hard for you to ask these questions of yourself.

Your words and actions set an example for the organization. Your personal credibility is critical. You have to say what you mean and do what you say. Nothing breeds cynicism and alienation more than an evident gap between your words and your deeds. There is no shortage of people who'll tell you what a great job you're doing. You need someone you can trust to tell you when your actions fall short of your words. If you aren't open to negative feedback, you can't address the words-deeds gap that undermines so many future-making efforts. But make your planners earn your trust, because it's probably better (certainly for you) to have no confidant than to have misplaced confidence.

For the Planner, Some Final Advice

Your value to the organization is measured in how well you help your boss do his or her job. Decisions will be made and actions will be taken, with or without you. It's not what you learn about the future that matters; it's what your boss learns about the future and the actions that he takes to prepare for that future. He's the future maker, not you. But you can help him do it.

A future-making boss will empower you by giving you direct access to him and a planning process to run. You must earn his confidence and trust, or the access will close, and the process will atrophy. The "care and feeding" of CEOs is both tough and tricky—each is different and you must adapt to them, not vice versa. You must play your role with respect, restraint, and discretion. But your job, by definition, risks confrontation because you often have to second-guess your boss's decisions and actions. Representing the future—the demand side of the future—is not a "yes-man's" job.

You must build your personal credibility. Speak only when you really have something to say. Learn how to say it right the first time. Don't talk too much. Maintain an outside-in perspective and focus on the demand side of the equation; your job is not to advocate solutions. Always apply the "value added" metric to what you say and do—"Am I helping my boss do his job and does he know it?" You want the CEO and others at the top to ask you what you think. You want them to listen when you speak. The limits of your job are defined by your personal credibility.

The more trust you earn, the more care you need to take. You need to question the futurity of the boss's decisions and provide a channel for negative feedback. If you get too wrapped up in the role of the top dog's confidant, you will lose perspective. You need to maintain a dispassionate, often analytic, distance to represent the future. Remember, the future doesn't care how well your boss is doing today. You can't be that indifferent—he is, after all, paying your salary—but you should try.

Note

1 Daniel Roth, "Quoted Often, Followed Rarely," *Fortune* (December 12, 2005), Fortune Archive online version, 2.

About the Author

CLARK A. MURDOCK, PH.D., is founder and president of the consulting firm, Murdock Associates, Inc., and a senior adviser at the non-partisan think tank, the Center for Strategic and International Studies. He provides consulting services in both the public and private sectors, directs and produces research on defense policy and organizational processes, and speaks in a wide variety of forums. An expert in the areas of strategic planning, defense policy and national security affairs, Dr. Murdock is the author or co-author of numerous publications, including *Beyond Goldwater-Nichols*, a multi-year study on reorganizing the U.S. government and the Department of Defense for the 21st century, and *Improving the Practice of National Security Strategy: A New Approach for the Post-Cold War World*.

Dr. Murdock has held numerous positions in government. He was the deputy director of strategic planning in the U.S. Air Force, the director of policy planning in the Office of the Secretary of Defense, and distinguished professor of military strategy at the National War College. He also served as policy adviser to the Chairman of the House Armed Services Committee, Les Aspin, and had a rotational tour on the staff of the National Security Council as one of President Ronald Reagan's senior directors. Before coming to Washington in 1979, he was a political science professor at the State University of New York at Buffalo, where he published his first book, *Defense Policy Formation: A Comparative Analysis of the McNamara Era*. He received his M.A. and Ph.D. from the University of Wisconsin-Madison and his B.A. from Swarthmore College.

Clark lives with his wife Kathleen on Maryland's Eastern Shore, overlooking the Chesapeake Bay. He is the father of three and the grandfather of five, and is a recovering golfer, now totally committed to gardening.